W9-AUF-610

Library of Congress Cataloging-in-Publication Data
Becoming a Coach: The CoachInc.com Approach / by Sandy Vilas
Includes index
ISBN 1-932466-00-2

Copy editing by Jennifer Corbin and Allison Wemyss
Layout and Design by Jennifer Corbin

Printed in the United States of America
10 9 8 7 6 5 4 3 2 1

Published by Coach U Press
PO Box 881595
Steamboat Springs, Colorado 80488

Becoming a Coach
The CoachInc.com Approach
Also: Making It As A Coach and How to Find a Coach
Sandy Vilas
Coach U Press

Printed in the United States by Morris Publishing
3212 East Highway 30
Kearney, NE 68847
1-800-650-7888

Becoming a Coach

The CoachInc.com Approach

by Sandy Vilas

This book is dedicated to the more than
26,000 people in over 50 countries
who have taken our training programs.
These people are making a difference
in the lives of thousands of people daily
and creating an incomparable life
for themselves in the process.

TABLE OF CONTENTS

INTRODUCTION

Thank you for your interest in coaching. We at CoachInc.com are so committed to this profession that we want to share it with everyone.

The *Becoming A Coach Handbook* is about what coaching is, why people work with a coach, why people choose the coaching profession and how to become a successful coach. This book is based on the perspectives of the thousands of individuals that CoachInc.com has trained worldwide, as well as our faculty and staff.

When you receive coach training at CoachInc.com, you will learn the basic coaching skills, not only to use with your clients and coachees, but also how to incorporate these skills in your day-to-day relationships with partners, customers, employees and friends. You will understand the powerful dynamic that occurs in coaching – the synergy that allows the coaching process to work.

In addition to teaching coaching skills, we also focus on practice development and personal development. We are considered to have the most extensive practice building materials and support in the industry. Another major benefit that students receive comes from the relationships they develop with other students and the faculty members – generally coaches are extremely generous, sharing their knowledge, wisdom, and experience.

Whether or not you choose to pursue coach training with us (and of course, we hope that you do) this book will help you better understand yourself and others, and gain a deep respect for the coaching profession.

In conclusion, we are extremely grateful to the dedicated, passionate and brilliant faculty, staff of CoachInc.com, who are the heart and soul of this company.

Sandy Vilas, MCC
CEO, CoachInc.com
Steamboat Springs, CO

Jennifer Corbin, PCC
President & COO, Coach U and Corporate Coach U
Solana Beach, CA

PART ONE

SECTION 1

An Overview Of CoachInc.Com

CoachInc.com has been training people to become masterful Life, Career and Business coaches for over a decade. Over 26,000 students and corporate managers have entered our training programs in order to enhance their coaching skill set. Our coach training programs, which are accredited by the International Coach Federation (ICF), provide individuals with broad coaching skills and numerous coaching models that they may apply in different areas.

All students begin their training with the Core Essentials Program (CEP), which gives students a basic foundation in coaching principles, ethics, skills, and practice development. This curriculum trains individuals in the Core Competencies, as set forth by the ICF, and will prepare students to proceed with advanced training, either as a personal and business coach, or as a corporate coach. The Core Essentials program meets the academic requirements for the Associated Certified Coach (ACC) certification through the ICF.

After completing the Core Essentials course, you can upgrade into one of our two advanced programs, the Advanced Coaching Program™ (ACP) or the Advanced Corporate Coaching Program™ (ACCP). In both these curricula, you'll have the opportunity to experience live coaching, both as the coach and the coachee, giving you practice in different kinds of coaching situations.

If you want to become a professional Coach -- or just develop exceptional coaching skills – the ACP will help you develop and refine your coaching skills. This comprehensive and effective training program focuses on personal development, for you and your coachees, working with different types of coachees, and building your own coaching practice. This program is required to become a Coach U

Certified Graduate (CUCG). This program designation, the CUCG, is accredited by the International Coach Federation (ICF).

If you wish to become a Corporate Coach, the ACCP will help you refine your organizational coaching skills and adapt them to a specific environment -- the corporation or other organization. This program is required to become a Corporate Coach U Certified Graduate (CCUCG). This program designation, the CCUCG, is also accredited by the International Coach Federation (ICF).

The International Coach Federation (ICF) is the oldest, largest and most-respected professional coaching association. CoachInc.com's training programs are fully accredited by the ICF. Our curriculum is based around the ICF's Core Competencies:

A. Setting the foundation

1. Meeting ethical guidelines and professional standards
2. Establishing the coaching agreement

B. Co-creating the relationship

1. Establishing trust and intimacy with the client
2. Coaching presence

C. Communicating effectively

1. Active listening
2. Powerful questioning
3. Direct communication

D. Facilitating learning and results

1. Creating awareness
2. Designing actions
3. Planning and goal setting
4. Managing progress and accountability

CoachInc.com also subscribes to, endorses, and trains all our students to operate according to the ICF's Code of Ethics, to ensure both the professionalism and integrity of the coaching profession. Because we believe so strongly in these principles, please look at the ethical standards for a coach:

1. I will conduct myself in a manner that reflects positively upon the coaching profession and I will refrain from engaging in conduct or making statements that may negatively impact the public's understanding or acceptance of coaching as a profession.

2. I will not knowingly make any public statements that are untrue or misleading, or make false claims in any written documents relating to the coaching profession.

3. I will respect different approaches to coaching. I will honor the efforts and contributions of others and not misrepresent them as my own.

4. I will be aware of any issues that may potentially lead to the misuse of my influence by recognizing the nature of coaching and the way in which it may affect the lives of others.

5. I will at all times strive to recognize personal issues that may impair, conflict or interfere with my coaching performance or my professional relationships. Whenever the facts and circumstances necessitate, I will promptly seek professional assistance and determine the action to be taken, including whether it is appropriate to suspend or terminate my coaching relationship(s).

6. As a trainer or supervisor of current and potential coaches, I will conduct myself in accordance with the ICF Code of Ethics in all training and supervisory situations.

7. I will conduct and report research with competence, honesty and within recognized scientific standards. My research will be carried out with the necessary approval or consent from those involved, and with an approach that will reasonably protect participants from any potential harm. All research efforts will be performed in a manner that complies with the laws of the country in which the research is conducted.

8. I will accurately create, maintain, store and dispose of any records of work done in relation to the practice of coaching in a way that promotes confidentiality and complies with any applicable laws.

9. I will use ICF member contact information (email addresses, telephone numbers, etc.) only in the manner and to the extent authorized by the ICF.

10. I will be responsible for setting clear, appropriate, and culturally sensitive boundaries that govern any physical contact that I may have with my clients.

11. I will not become sexually involved with any of my clients.

12. I will construct clear agreements with my clients, and will honor all agreements made in the context of professional coaching relationships.

13. I will ensure that, prior to or at the initial session, my coaching client understands the nature of coaching,

the bounds of confidentiality, financial arrangements and other terms of the coaching agreement.

14. I will accurately identify my qualifications, expertise and experience as a coach.

15. I will not intentionally mislead or make false claims about what my client will receive from the coaching process or from me as their coach.

16. I will not give my clients or prospective clients information or advice I know or believe to be misleading.

17. I will not knowingly exploit any aspect of the coach-client relationship for my personal, professional or monetary advantage or benefit.

18. I will respect the client's right to terminate coaching at any point during the process. I will be alert to indications that the client is no longer benefiting from our coaching relationship.

19. If I believe the client would be better served by another coach, or by another resource, I will encourage the client to make a change.

20. I will suggest that my clients seek the services of other professionals when deemed appropriate or necessary.

21. I will take all reasonable steps to notify the appropriate authorities in the event a client discloses an intention to endanger self or others.

22. I will respect the confidentiality of my client's information, except as otherwise authorized by my client, or as required by law.

23. I will obtain agreement from my clients before releasing their names as clients or references, or any other client identifying information.

24. I will obtain agreement from the person being coached before releasing information to another person compensating me.

25. I will seek to avoid conflicts between my interests and the interests of my clients.

26. Whenever any actual conflict of interest or the potential for a conflict of interest arises, I will openly disclose it and fully discuss with my client how to deal with it in whatever way best serves my client.

27. I will disclose to my client all anticipated compensation from third parties that I may receive for referrals of that client.

28. I will only barter for services, goods or other non-monetary remuneration when it will not impair the coaching relationship.

We at CoachInc.com believe that we have the finest, most comprehensive coach training programs in the world. We use the most up-to-date materials in the industry, and John Wiley & Sons, a worldwide publisher, has just published our curriculum in three volumes:

The ***Coach U Personal and Corporate Coach Training Handbook*** contains the basic information that you'll need to become an effective coach. The book includes a detailed explanation of each of the core coaching skills, incorporating advantages, pitfalls, and exercises that reinforce using those skills. In addition, this handbook includes information on how to set up, manage and market a successful coaching practice.

The **Coach U Personal Development Workbook and Guide** contains the tools you need to build your personal foundation—preparing yourself to successfully coach others, and perhaps just as important, how to create a more fulfilled life. This includes an awareness of what is working (and what is not) in your life, living according to your own values, establishing boundaries, and getting rid of tolerations (the things that sap your energy and prevent you from living a great life). The Personal Foundation course helps students to develop the critical tools necessary to become a truly effective and successful coach.

The ***Coach U Essential Coaching Tools Book and CD*** includes a wealth of material that a coach needs for a successful coaching practice. It includes self-assessment tools, worksheets and exercises to use with your clients, and marketing and business materials to help you set up and run a profitable coaching practice or provide superior coaching within an organization.

"Enroll in Coach U or Corporate Coach U to learn the best strategies on how to build a successful and sustainable coaching business. It took me nine months to build a practice of 80 clients, so I know it can be done".
Sandy Vilas, MCC, CEO of CoachInc.com

Completing any of our advanced programs satisfies the training component for the ICF's Professional Certified Coach (PCC) and Master Certified Coach (MCC) designations. This means that once you have completed your training, logged the required client hours, demonstrated coaching competencies, and a few additional requirements, you'll be eligible for these ICF certifications. All of our faculty members hold PCC or MCC certifications to ensure that you are trained by qualified, experienced and certified professionals. If, for any reason, you choose not to receive your training from us, make sure that you receive your training through an ICF-accredited program.

The decision to become a coach or to integrate coaching skills and competencies into your personal and professional life is an important one. Many of our students and graduates tell us that if they had received our coach training earlier in their lives, they may have been able to accomplish what they wanted more easily and with less stress. Both personally and professionally, our students and graduates are amazed at the results that they are able to achieve in their own lives and the lives of others through coaching.

CoachInc.com's Guiding Principles

In order to get the most out of this book, we feel that we should provide some context to coaching using the CoachInc.com approach. These principles are basic understandings of how people behave and interact, and how coaching facilitates collaboration, creativity, innovation, action and results. As you read the Guiding Principles, you will begin to understand the values and beliefs that are the core of our training. Effective coaching helps create an environment where people create results that exceed expectations - sometimes even their own.

For a printable version of our Guiding Principles, please visit our website at www.coachinc.com and click on "Guiding Principles" located on the center bar.

The core values of CoachInc.com are integrity, heart-centeredness, truth, wisdom, generosity and quality. These values, our Guiding Principles, are the bedrock of our company and the basis for the experience our students enjoy at CoachInc.com.
Sandy Vilas, MCC, United States

The next page shows our Guiding Principles in table format.

Guiding Principles	Coach U	Corporate Coach U
People have something in common	We return to our common connections by loving, honoring and valuing ourselves and others.	People are drawn together in companies through a compelling mission and shared values.
People are inquisitive	Wonder, curiosity and inquiry are the source of all learning.	Organizations that encourage curiosity accelerate learning and creativity
People contribute	Contribution based on purpose generates true fulfillment.	When organizations recognize individual contribution, they grow leaders at every level.
People grow from connection	Connection is the wellspring of creativity.	Collaboration is a conduit for enhancing people's strengths and generating innovative solutions.
People seek value	Listening provides an ever-present access to value.	Listening beyond words is the currency of valuing human capital.
People act in their own interest	Discernment reveals the opportunities in every situation.	When people make the shift from self-interest to self-responsibility, it enhances the quality of interaction with colleagues and clients.
People live from their perception	An inclusive, present-based perception of reality is the platform for effective action.	Recognizing that people perceive reality through their own filters leads to effective communication and creates a platform for positive action.
People have a choice	Awareness is the precursor to choice.	Shifting perspectives expand awareness and reveal new choices.
People define their own integrity	The vigilant development of the fit between conduct and calling creates integrity.	Integrity for individuals comes from continuous alignment between the organization's mission, vision, and values, and their own.

SECTION 2

Should I Receive Coach Training?

We've heard from the thousands of people trained at CoachInc.com that they have always wanted to help people and have always felt like coaches. They were the ones people turned to for help or support, because they always knew just what to say to help a friend or family member through a rough period in their personal or professional life. And, they were the ones who enjoyed helping others think bigger, broader, smarter and differently.

People interact, motivate, create and innovate when they are understood, empowered, motivated, focused and clear about what it is they want to do. Many people enroll in our training programs because they have assisted others in the past and want to learn how to facilitate the development of others while gaining a new skill set.

Does any of this sound like you?

To be sure that learning coaching skills is the right choice for you, please read the following statements and place a checkmark if the statement is true for you. (Please note that some of the statements are more revealing than may appear.)

- I sense things about others that they are surprised about when I share with them.
- I am intuitive and can sense things about people that other people may not.
- I enjoy helping others solve a problem with which they are struggling.
- I've got a spark. People comment on how alive I am.
- I am a very positive person.

- I am naturally curious about people. I want to learn about them.
- I am fascinated about life and how it all works.
- I am excited about the significant changes occurring in all areas of life today and want to stay ahead of the curve.
- I am willing to be honest with people, even if it's awkward for me or for them.
- I deeply respect people and accept very different ways of thinking/living.
- I enjoy being a strategist. I like helping people chart a course.
- I have special abilities and I believe that people are willing to pay for them.
- I am willing to take the time to learn and perfect the craft of coaching.
- I attract people who want my support and input.
- I am open to learning new concepts and paradigms, even if they don't make sense at first.
- I can handle paradoxes.
- I am willing to have my life be a model for others.
- I am willing to charge for my time and services (if I become a professional coach).
- I enjoy adding value to whomever I can, because I enjoy serving others.
- I am aware of my limits, yet I know I can coach others well.
- I want to learn new coaching models and technologies to help enhance my skill set and the performance of others.
- I am willing to learn coaching skills via TeleClass discussions and self-study.
- I am willing to immerse myself in learning to be a masterful coach.
- I care a lot about other people and enjoy seeing them achieve their goals.

- I am excited about sharing what I've learned with others, and am willing to fashion it into something that fits the other person's needs perfectly.

Scoring Key

20-25	You are already a coach; formal training will enhance your natural strengths.
15-19	You are an excellent candidate to become a coach
10-14	Although coaching may not be the right career for you, learning coaching skills will certainly improve your current work and quality of life.
0-9	It appears that coaching would not be the right choice for you.

Summing Up...

How did you do? Most people who read this book score 15 or above. If that's you, please give serious consideration to becoming a coach, or, if you're already coaching, to taking your skill set and practice to the next level by participating in one of our coach training programs.

SECTION 3

Who Are Coachinc.com's Students And Graduates?

Coaching is very attractive to individuals with already successful careers, perhaps because it gives people an opportunity to do what they most want to do – help others grow. Because the coaching profession has only been around for about fifteen years, most of us didn't know that coaching was an option when we planned our careers.

Who becomes an independent professional coach?

There are thousands of occupations in the world today, and coaches come from virtually all of them. It's common to see consultants, therapists, trainers, human resource professionals, healing arts professionals and all types of managers transition into coaching. And, it's not uncommon for attorneys, accountants, business owners, engineers and even ministers to enter the field of coaching. Coaching skills benefit everyone who works with other people and wants to achieve better results.

What if I don't intend to become an independent professional coach?

During the last several years at CoachInc.com, we have noticed that at least 40% of our students plan to continue in their current professions with a competitive edge, or continue working with their current employers in a different way. With training in coaching skills, they learn to incorporate their new skills, models, techniques and technology into their professional lives.

For example, some therapists add coaching to their menu of counseling services, whereas other therapists migrate completely to coaching. A manager who wants to better manage and motivate staff might enroll in one of CoachInc.com's programs to improve his or her communication and management skills. He or she will also learn how to coach others and how to develop leadership skills in others.

"Everyone benefits from learning coaching skills because they can be used in virtually any personal, business or corporate situation. It's all about working smarter, not harder, in an ever-changing world."
– Jennifer Corbin, PCC , United States

Where are coaches coming from?

Coaching is a viable career option and most coaches come from other professions and career tracks. Other people who enter our programs are coaches without training who want to improve their skills and become certified coaches.

Some CoachInc.com students are in career transition and begin building coaching practices while they study. Others are happy in their careers and will add coaching skills to their repertoire. Some work part-time as coaches, while working in another field. Others transition out of the corporate arena to become full-time coaches before they retire.

Business schools, corporations and prominent national magazines recognize the value of coaching in any personal or organizational environment. CoachInc.com's training programs and resources add attractive, marketable skills to any resume or curriculum vitae.

As a successful corporate employee, I was professional, respected, and remunerated, yet not fulfilled. Coach U's Advanced Coach Training Program was a turning point in my life as it addresses the 'whole person'. Now I've integrated my professional skills with

my own personal development, and for the first time in my life I feel on purpose.
- Belinda Merry, PCC, Australia

Why are Healthcare and Healing Professionals learning coaching skills?

Physicians, dentists, nurses, chiropractors, physical therapists, massage therapists, and personal trainers usually coach part-time or integrate their coaching skills in their practices to help them better understand human behavior, communicate more effectively with their patients and clients to further their progress, and build teamwork among their staff.

"As a massage therapist, I blend my extensive knowledge of the physical, emotional and energetic aspects with my coaching skills to help both my massage clients and coachees move forward."
– Kathy Pike, United States

Why are Professional Service Providers becoming coaches?

Half the professionals who take coach training, including attorneys, accountants, realtors, brokers, insurance agents, professional organizers, business consultants and computer consultants migrate from their current profession to becoming full-time coaches within four years. The other half continues in their profession, but benefit from coach training to assist their clients more effectively, in less time, and also strengthen their own Personal Foundation in order to become more productive, avoid burnout and generate higher incomes.

"As a real estate speaker and trainer, my coaching skills increase my value to my audiences. By modeling the coaching skills, real estate people can discover what their clients really want and help them achieve it."
– Joeann Fossland, United States

How does coach training strengthen Business and Personal Consultants?

Consultants include those working in the areas of management, small business and executive consulting, organizational development, industrial psychologists, marketing consultants and others. Consultants use their coaching skills to enjoy a more rewarding, long-term, lucrative, and less stressful professional life.

The skills and tools I have acquired at Corporate Coach U have enabled me to develop my own practice supporting small business owners very quickly. The new Wiley textbooks support my continual development and provide a quick reference guide and fantastic place to 'dip' for reminders.
- Hilary J Oliver, United Kingdom

"I worked with Fortune 100 companies for 13 years before becoming a full-time coach. As a consultant, clients often failed to fully implement our recommendations, because they were other people's answers, but using a coach approach, clients create their own solutions, and felt empowered by the process."
– Meryl Moritz, United States

Why do Corporate Employees learn coaching skills?

A corporate employee might be a manager, executive or CEO. Perhaps he or she works in human relations, as an executive director, project manager or sales professional. Corporate employees learn coaching skills to become more effective with their staff, create a more effective and empowering corporate culture, and help their staff develop professionally.

I graduated the Corporate Coach Program in 2003, and it radically changed my attitude. I used to be a workaholic, and very impatient about others' performance, but I didn't know how to help people improve. Corporate Coach U taught me how to be a coach rather than just a boss.
- Helen Hyonsook Ko, South Korea

Our Advanced Corporate Coaching Program is especially designed for Executives, CEOs, Managers and Business Leaders, who want to get well trained as a coach or to integrate coaching into their leadership style. Please visit www.ccui.com to learn more.

Organizations now recognize the importance of providing mangers with the tools they need to help their people develop their full potential. Research tells us that the number one reason people look for new jobs is their relationship with their immediate supervisor. The data also identifies the key factors in employee retention to be job satisfaction and the opportunity for professional development.

Continually revised and updated, the Coaching Clinic® has been equipping managers around the globe with the model and skills needed to create a collaborative and developmental culture for almost a decade.

Cheryl Smith, MA, Master Certified Coach
Director Coaching Clinic Programs
Corporate Coach U

Why do Independent and Creative People enroll in programs at CoachInc.com?

Many of our students are highly creative or independent people such as entrepreneurs, small business owners, actors, dancers, singers, writers, engineers, scientists, researchers and architects. They come to CoachInc.com to add coaching to their career repertoire, build a steady income stream, and help others design and implement a more creative and fulfilling life.

"As a performing artist, becoming a coach was a natural next step for me. For me, coaching is another form of artful expression. The 'dance' with the coachee is incredibly inspiring and creative. Thanks, Coach U."
– Pamela Richarde, MCC, United States

Why do Helping Professionals integrate coaching skills?

The helping professions include counseling, therapy, psychology, ministry and others. After receiving coach training, many therapists and counselors enjoy a better and more productive relationship with their clients, empowering them to be responsible for their own lives rather than trying to "fix" their problems. Coaching also gives them higher fees, as well as the convenience and flexibility of working at any time from any place.

"CoachInc.com's courses provided a solid training to become a professional coach, which allows me to significantly make a difference for my clients both personally and professionally. For myself, everyday is joyful and I am more authentic, fully expressed and fulfilled. Life could not be more perfect!"
- Lynda Aurora, MCC, China

"For years, I'd been looking for a good coaching school in Holland. For the last five years I've been coaching women entrepreneurs, but didn't have coach training. When I found out about Coach U and looked at their website, I immediately registered for the Core Essentials Program, which I took in March 2005. I'm now building my coaching business and looking forward to creating a solid coaching community in Holland!"
- Ingeborg van Meggelen, Holland

Why do Trainers, Presenters, Speakers and Educators seek coaching skills training?

Those who train and motivate people can benefit from learning coaching skills, because it helps them work more effectively with groups, provides a stable and consistent income stream, and builds their network.

"Using [coaching] instead of sending executives and managers to seminars two or three times a year can be more beneficial to ongoing career development."
– PC Week

What personal backgrounds do coaches come from?

In addition to the aforementioned career tracks, coaches also come from various backgrounds, or have specialized skill sets or special life experiences.

Single Parents

"As a single parent and a coach, my schedule allows me to attend school activities and extra-curricular events."
– Sandra Dell, United States

Those With Diverse Interests

"Writing and lapidary and personal growth are my passions, and Coach U taught me how to combine them, with the skills necessary to make it work"
– Edmond E. Frank, United States

The Unconventional

"My interests were so eclectic, I thought I'd never fit in anywhere. Coaching gave me a way to use everything I'm interested in-- from golf to the Beatles, from Shakespeare to Seinfeld-- to help my coachees."
– Jay Perry, MCC, United States

The Personal Growth-Oriented

"Although I've been involved in personal growth, I didn't know how to integrate my beliefs into my life. Coach U provided the guidance, structure, accountability and ongoing support of a community that certainly lives its teachings..."
– Judy Godinez, United States

The Spiritually-Centered

"Coach U allows me to operate in the material world, while honoring and developing my own spirituality and that of my coachees."
– Keith Collins, United States

People Who Enjoy Transformation

"Coach U is essential for anyone who wants to transform his or her life."
– Sharon Hooper, PCC, United States

The Highly Motivated

"As a coach, I can motivate people by pulling them forward instead of pushing them from behind"
– Dawn M. Osborn, United States

Early Adopters

"Coaching plays a vital role in an organization's ability to continuously transform itself to meet tomorrow's challenges."
– Pam Butterfield, United States

The Highly Creative

"Creative people often want brainstorming partners and sounding boards and need a space to explore ideas and to get support when it seems in short supply elsewhere."
- Ted Isensee, United States

High Performer/Superstar

"In my former career, I was a high performer, but as a coach I've learned to let go of the need for perfection. I now have even more energy since I don't push myself so hard."
– Natalie Gahrmann, ACC, United States

Athlete

"As an athlete, I spent many years developing my physical abilities, and as a coach I often refer to my outdoor adventures to provide inspire and transform others. It all came together."
- Kathy Pike, United States

Creator/Inventor

"I had a dozen projects in the works at one time, but couldn't focus on any one project. My coach helped me organize each project and now I produce more than I ever dreamed. I could."
– Jane Yousey, United States

What demographic groups do coaches come from?

Baby Boomer

"As baby boomers near retirement our focus is shifting from career success and material wealth to making a difference in the world. Coach training offers the opportunity to investigate these questions."
– Cynthia Bahnuik, Canada

Gen Xer

"I was struggling with finding a satisfying career. Coaching has all my 'ideal career elements.' I now coach people who are looking for their perfect work, like I once was. It's the ideal situation."
– Lucinda Kerschensteiner, United States

Retiree

"I am 60 years old and retiring from my landscape design business, but needed something stimulating, engaging and creative, and flexible. Becoming a coach was perfect for me."
– Michael Sheffield, United States

What educational background should a coach have?

A high percentage of coaches have at least a bachelor's degree and over half have an advanced degree. A strong educational background is an advantage, however, life experience and the willingness to learn is even more important than what you already know.

Ten years ago I made a new start in life! I was sixty two years of age and had been a clinical social worker and psychotherapist for at least one lifetime, if not two. Being a professional coach fulfills my personal mission and fully utilizes my greatest gifts and talent. As an extra bonus, Coach U is my extended family -- connections of this quality and duration are fabulous.
- Harriett Simon Salinger, MCC, United States

Summing Up…

Did you identify yourself anywhere in this section? Our coaches do a much better job at telling you who they are and why they became coaches. People with very diverse educational, demographic, personal and professional backgrounds have joined CoachInc.com programs to become more skillful at coaching.

SECTION 4

What Are the Benefits of Becoming a Professional Coach?

1. Coaching is a rewarding and fulfilling career choice.

Coaches LOVE what they do because they enjoy helping people get what they most want in life. Just think about it – you work with positive people who are eager to learn and achieve. They want your support and the benefits of your training and are willing to pay for it.

"The greatest benefit to me of being a coach is that I can gather all my skills, values, talents and past experiences and wrap them into a package that is fun, challenging, helpful to others and pays well, too."
– Jo Ann Heiser, United States

2. Coaches enjoy the freedom to live and work anywhere they wish.

Coaches can coach from their homes, an outside office or while traveling. Because coaching can be done by telephone, location and geographical boundaries become irrelevant. A coaching practice is portable so if you move or travel the country in an RV, you can coach your clients.

"Quality of life really increases when you can travel abroad while maintaining your coaching practice. My clients get an extra dose of 'motivation' when they hear I'm coaching from the Great Barrier Reef or another great location."
- Jennifer Corbin, PCC, United States

3. Being a coach accelerates your personal and professional development.

If you enjoy developing yourself and understand the value of ongoing learning, you'll enjoy being a coach because you're in an environment that encourages growth. Because your coachees are on a fast track, your pace is naturally accelerated, because you learn from each other. It's that simple.

"As an engineer and technical project manager, I thought I was coaching when I ***gave*** *people what I thought were the answers. The Advanced program totally shifted my way of working with people. Now, I work with other technical professionals to enhance their leadership and coaching skills to make the workplace more effective and fun. They prefer this approach..."*
- Christel Cherry, United States

4. A coaching business has the potential to quickly bring in a high income.

Coaches in private practice average $175 an hour in coaching fees, with the range being between $150 and $300 per hour. Because coaching is so effective, coachees can achieve significant results in as little as 30 minutes a week with you. So, if you charge them $350 a month (the national average for experienced coaches), you'll work with each coachee for two hours a month, for an average of $175 an hour.

5. You will flourish in an expanded professional network and community.

Success today is largely dependent on the size and strength of your personal and professional network. The more people you get to know – and who get to know you – the better for your long-term financial success and professional development. As a coach, you instantly expand your network given the cooperative and collaborative way coaches interact. In fact, our students tell us that one of the greatest advantages of training at CoachInc.com is the personal and professional relationships that they have made.

"The Core Essentials Program provides the structure that enables me to deliver a higher level of professionalism and quality service. Being able to tap into the collective wisdom of literally thousands of masterful coaches has significantly improved the quality of support I provide."
- James Summers, United States

6. New coaches enter the profession easily and proceed at their own pace.

You do not need to take 3 years off and become a full-time student to become a coach. You can stay in your current profession and learn at your own pace. You can complete core training in as little as one year or take up to three years – it's entirely up to you.

7. You can truly earn while you learn.

Many coaches start coaching within the six months of entering our training programs and most are earning fees shortly thereafter. It's very important to coach while you learn and learn while you coach. And, while you're at it, why not enjoy the financial rewards that come when you add tremendous value to others?

"Within a month of joining Coach U, I had 5 paying coachees. Although they only paid me $30 a month, within a short time, I charged ten times that fee."
- Michele Lisenbury Christensen, PCC, USA

8. Coaching is a way to make a difference in others' lives.

Coaches like helping others improve the quality of their lives and achieve their goals. Many of our students have always wanted to make a difference in this world, and being a coach lets them see the impact they have on other peoples' lives.

9. Their chosen profession brings coaches great joy.

When you feel better at the end of a day than you did at the start of the day, joy is likely present. Coaching invigorates both parties – thanks to synergy, it creates energy, and becomes even more joyful.

"The Corporate Coach U program and my mentor coach program had a tremendous effect on my private and business life. It helped me discover my real passion: supporting others to change and improve their life or career."
- Ruud Baanders, Netherlands

10. Coaching is a platform from which to launch yourself, if desired.

When you learn coaching skills and take your personal and professional development to the next level, you may develop a local, regional, national and even international reputation. This gives you many options – writing a book, teaching TeleClasses or live trainings, publishing e-newsletters, forming communities, getting business invitations from others and more.

Several CoachInc.com graduates are popular authors. Oprah! featured Coach U graduate Laura Berman Fortgang, author of *Take Yourself to the Top: Secrets of America's #1 Career Coach*, and Cheryl Richardson, who also appeared on Oprah, wrote *Take Time for Your Life*, as well as other best-selling books.

"Coach U's Advanced Coaching Program, which combines coach training, personal development and business development, has surpassed all my expectations. Coach U is also committed to continuous improvement by adding new classes, revamped curriculum, user-friendly website, and professional, easy-to-use textbooks. The emphasis on personal and practice development serves me and my clients to achieve success."
- Grace Durfee, PCC, United States

"The Coaching Clinic Certification affords a breadth of communication skills and tools. As a high achiever and developer, I gravitate towards cultures I can challenge and motivate to reach their highest potential. After purchasing the three new Coach U textbooks, I'm reviewing Core Essentials enrollment, another step towards financial independence and lifelong learning."
- John Mooney, United States

Summing Up...

Everyone has his or her own reasons for becoming a coach, but almost every coach enjoys the ten benefits just outlined. The question to ask yourself is how you would benefit by becoming a coach.

Perhaps the most exciting benefit is that you can identify and work with your Ideal Client/Coachee. What personality traits would they have? What do they want out of life? What past experiences have they had? What motivates them? What do they want to accomplish? What is most important to them? Answering these questions will help you know exactly who you can start coaching right away.

SECTION 5

Why Does A Person Hire A Coach?

Coaches are successful because people have heard great things about coaching and want to hire a coach. Most people don't need to be sold on the idea of having a coach – they either clearly see the value for themselves or they don't. Here are the most common reasons why people hire a coach:

To set better goals.

A goal that reflects your true values is a joy to work toward and reach. However, the wrong goal – perhaps based on whims, advertising, other people's agendas or instant gratification – takes needless effort and often comes at a high cost to your body and your soul. Coaches help people discover what they really want, using the coachee's own values, needs and vision as personal reference points.

To reach their goals faster.

Who doesn't want to reach their goals faster, with less stress? A coach gives consistent support and offers innovative strategies and approaches to help people quickly reach their goals. CoachInc.com trained coaches are familiar with Performance and Attraction Approach models and share these with their coachees.

To make significant changes.

If you're human, you make changes every day, given the rapid rate of change in every aspect of life, business and technology. A coach is uniquely trained to help you make fundamental and permanent changes in your personal and professional life.

To become more financially successful.

Most coachees want to build enough financial reserves to fund the lifestyle they want. Coaches are not financial planners, but they know about adding value, which is the source of financial independence for most individuals. A coach can also help you adjust your spending and lifestyle in order to create a better financial future.

To design – and live – your best life.

Is it possible to have your ideal life? Certainly. Every day, coaches help thousands of people improve their lives. It is part of our job and a source of our joy because coaches help people understand that they can have it all.

To get ahead professionally.

There are many ways to get ahead today in your career, profession or small business. CoachInc.com coaches know the most effective ways to advance your career, build your reputation and develop your business.

To make better decisions.

As life speeds up and becomes a smorgasbord, we are presented with far more choices than our parents ever had, but who had Decision-Making 101 in high school or college? A coach can teach you to make the best decisions for you, regardless of the circumstances.

To have someone to collaborate with.

When you have someone to brainstorm with, what you end up with is synergy, which is essential for success in the next decade. Without it, your creativity is limited; with it, creativity and innovation comes easily. The coach is a high-benefit, low-cost collaborative partner.

To improve their relationships and family.

The more virtual the world gets, the more important your relationships become. Strengthening your family and attracting and maintaining friendships are essential to providing meaning, support and love in your life. Your coach can help you improve your communication and relating skills and attract the best people to you.

To make a bigger impact in the world.

Want to make your mark in this life or make a difference on the planet? People work with coaches to identify and use their unique strengths to make a difference, without the traditionally high emotional or physical cost of leadership.

To simplify their lives.

Can you really have it all and still simplify your life? Absolutely! CoachInc.com coaches use proprietary coaching models, methods and technologies that help people to simplify, yet also enrich their life.

To strengthen their Personal Foundation.

It is impressive to see the number of coachees who want to strengthen themselves from the inside out. They know that external support and motivation is helpful, but if they strengthen their Personal Foundation, they will have a much stronger and more resilient base from which to succeed. CoachInc.com coaches may offer the Personal Foundation Program to their coachees.

To reduce stress and tolerations.

Stress comes with our times, but many people realize that the cost of this stress is too high and hire a coach to help them identify and reduce their personal stress levels. Many CoachInc.com trained coaches also use the Toleration-Free

Approach to identify the things that drain your energy in order to reduce your stress level.

To increase income or revenue.

Seeking to get a raise or build your business? A coach can help you craft a career or marketing strategy. CoachInc.com trained coaches have learned dozens of such strategies to help you increase your income or revenue.

To become a better manager, executive or businessperson.

Many coaches are former managers, executives or business owners from virtually every field and industry. They can help you strengthen your management, leadership or entrepreneurial skills because they've been there and they understand where you're coming from.

Summing Up...

As you've read, there are many good reasons to hire a coach, but you might be wondering how you can become a coach if you don't know everything described above.

There are two things you should know. First, our basic Core Essentials Program will teach you the skills you can use in these areas. Then, by selecting the Advanced Coaching Program or Advanced Corporate Coaching Program, you can enhance and practice these skills, enabling you to handle virtually any coaching scenario that arises. We will give you the information, strategies and models you need, which are not hard to learn. Second, since coachees hire you because they feel that your personality, style, strengths and approach suits them, you probably already have a lot of what they need.

SECTION 6

How Does A Coach Work With People?

Now that you understand the focus of a coaching relationship, you may wonder what the coach does during a typical coaching session. In fact, we are often asked by prospective students what they will actually do that makes the coach worth $175 to $300 per hour. Here are the most common things that a coach does, and why it matters.

A coach listens.

When is the last time someone completely listened to you so perfectly that you felt fully heard? When a coach listens, they hear you, not just your current situation. And when you feel heard, you can hear yourself. That's worth a lot. As part of our curriculum, new coaches learn critical listening. Through study, practice and feedback, they become highly attuned listeners who hear much more than is actually said.

A coach lends support.

Does an Olympic skater attempt to win the gold medal by herself? No, she's smart enough to find the right coach who will bring out her personal best. Recently, people have become willing to reach out and find support while they make changes, solve problems, and evaluate challenges. This is no longer a sign of weakness; it's a sign of intelligence.

A coach often challenges their coachees.

If you look back at your life, you can probably think of three people who challenged you to take a chance, invest in yourself or make a big change. You may have felt stressed then, but are now grateful for the courage and care it took for those people to challenge you. Every day, coaches do this for their coachees, because they want the people they work with to look back five years later and say, "Thank goodness my coach had the foresight to nudge me back then!" Our students learn when, where and how to challenge their coachees, for maximum long-term benefit, and also to make challenges in a way that the coachee feels empowered to accept, decline, or make a counter-offer.

A coach is motivational.

Humans being human and life being life, we all need help staying focused and motivated. The coach provides this because people may need the occasional pep talk, encouragement or inspiration – some people may want all of this at different times throughout the coaching relationship.

Whatever flavor of motivation someone needs, a coach can provide it. Remember, people who hire a coach are up to great things and encouragement is an important ingredient in their success. After all, we are human.

A coach guides the coachee.

Life used to be pretty simple. Most people chose a career and lifestyle and simply followed it – or fought it. But over the past 30 years, we've realized that there is no single correct path, and that we can follow whichever path we choose. Yet, we were never taught how to create a path that's joyful, prosperous and balanced.

That's where the coach can help by discovering what coachees most want, and offering the perspective, wisdom and reference points that help make their lives more fulfilling, successful and rewarding. Our coaches receive extensive training in the life planning process... and as a part of their training, they develop their own life plans.

A coach collaborates with coachees.

Synergy is what occurs when two people collaborate, and that's exactly what coaches do. Coaches are active co-creators with their coachees, not just passive listeners. Most individuals or companies hire a coach because they see the value in a having a third eye, sounding board or creative partner to help them achieve what they most want, in the easiest, most enjoyable manner.

A coach evolves his or her coachees.

Humans are evolving, just like every other form of life. We may call it professional development, personal growth or transformation, but these are all part of our personal evolution. Although most coachees don't ask for personal evolution, they know they want to develop themselves in new ways. As a coach, you can help people evolve.

A coach asks powerful questions.

One of the best ways to provide value to a coachee is to ask the right question at the right time in the right manner. We call these Laser Questions – fundamental questions that cut to the core of the matter and get the coachee thinking bigger and better. A single question – if it's the right one – can be worth tens of thousands of dollars to a coachee. Every one of our coaches is thoroughly trained in the skill of questioning.

A coach understands.

The coach is expected to be understanding – patient, caring and respectful of the coachee – and also be a professional who understands the dynamic of virtually any situation, problem or choice that a coachee is facing. Both individuals and teams in organizations want to work with a coach who can help them make sense of what's going on, so they can start working on a solution. Our coaches learn coaching skills and competencies that can be applied to common coachee situations.

A coach strategizes.

One of the roles of a coach is to help the coachee identify the best and easiest way to accomplish something or solve a problem. In other words, you help the coachee to answer the question, "How will I achieve that?" It might surprise you to know that there are only about 30 strategies that a coach needs to know in order to be an effective strategist. Once you learn these strategies, you can empower others to use them effectively in virtually any situation. Strategies also give you a competitive advantage in the marketplace, by making your coaching that much more effective and practical.

Summing up...

Coaching is really an advanced form of relating. Thus, a coach develops scores of specialized listening, communication and relating skills to help coachees identify what they want, clarify who they are and develop strategies to reach their goals.

There is no mystery to the coaching process, but it does take between 18-36 months to master professional coaching skills. If that sounds like a long time, it's because you not only learn and practice the skill, but you also evolve yourself internally in order to use your skills with a wide range of coachees. Coaching is a sophisticated process and coachees expect their coaches to thoroughly understand how to use their skills.

SECTION 7

What Tools Do Coaches Use In Their Work?

Every profession has its own set of tools and specialized knowledge. For example, an accountant uses a calculator and accounting software, a chiropractor uses his hands and knowledge of the body and an optometrist uses lenses and other optical equipment. So, it makes sense that coaches have their own set of tools. The Coach U Essential Coaching Tools Book has all the tools and assessments you'll need. The most common coaching tools are:

1. Self-assessment checklists.

Most coachees want to learn and understand more about themselves and how they operate in life. CoachInc.com trained coaches have access to over 100 self-assessments and coaching forms (developed at Coach U) that they can share with coachees. These tools help coachees discover and fulfill their personal needs, articulate their true values, accelerate their personal development, identify and eliminate conditions they're suffering from, strengthen their Personal Foundation, and more. The more the coachee learns about him or herself, the more he or she will benefit from coaching.

2. Coachee programs.

Close to 100,000 individuals, teams, business leaders, and organizations have benefited from being coached by CoachInc.com coaches. We have developed programs both for individuals and businesses. Some programs are 100-point checklists such as the New Business Start-Up or Super Reserve Programs, while others are learning modules such as

The Attraction Program or The Personal Foundation Program. With these programs, you won't need to reinvent the wheel.

3. Success principles.

Most coachees want to learn how to become more successful. The CoachInc.com coach has a comprehensive collection of what we call Success Principles. When coaches learn and integrate these principles into their own knowledge base, they have that much more to offer coachees.

4. Coaching models.

Building on the Success Principle, CoachInc.com has developed dozens of Coaching Models. Because Coaching Models give coaches a visual representation of a situation or strategy, they can help their coachees to reach their goals much more quickly. Some of the most popular models are the 123 Coach! Model, the S-Five Model, the Who/What/How Model and the Five-Step Coaching Conversation.

Summing Up...

As you can see, coaching is a lot more than just motivating and supporting your coachees. There is a technology and methodology to coaching. The process is easy to learn because as you progress through your training and learn coaching skills, you also become familiar with the coaching tools to help you apply those new skills.

SECTION 8

The CoachInc.com Approach

By now, you probably have a good idea whether coach training is right for you now. In this section, we describe the special approach that CoachInc.com uses in its training. You'll read about our philosophy, our effective training systems, the unique culture at CoachInc.com, our coaching methodology, and the sort of person who invests in a CoachInc.com training program.

How does CoachInc.com train coaches?

CoachInc.com has developed an innovative system for training coaches to be highly effective. Here is how and why it works so well.

1. Having the right colleagues.

You learn how to coach well by surrounding yourself with coaches who have similar personal and educational backgrounds. There are not only different coaching styles among coaches, but also varying degrees of experience and expertise. In other words, not all coaches are fully trained or take the time to master their craft, so it's important to join a community of coaches who ARE personally committed and intellectually able to master this craft. One of the things you'll find at CoachInc.com is a student body eager and able to learn.

2. Using CoachInc.com coaching models.

You learn how to coach well by starting with the Three-Step Universal Coaching Model™ (Who/What/How), the S-Five Model and the Five-Step Coaching Conversation. As complex as coachees can be, the coaching process is fairly simple. CoachInc.com invented the Universal Coaching

Model, which is the easiest to learn and most powerful coaching model available today.

In our view, the coaching process is about: a) helping coachees discover and understand who they are (who); b) helping coachees identify and clarify what they most want (what); and c) helping coachees create and develop strategies to achieve their goals (how). Unless the what and how are integrated with the individual (who), what and how will take longer to accomplish, and certainly will not bring the high levels of happiness and fulfillment that are possible.

What's powerful about the Universal Coaching Model is that it's not linear. Depending on the coachee, you can start at any point during the coaching process.

3. Understanding people.

You learn how to coach well by understanding what motivates us, how we operate and what it takes to be successful in life. Specifically, a coach knows about personal needs, the seven stages of development, developmental accelerators, the reduction of resistance, the role of environments, core values, sources of motivation, cultural differences, belief systems, assumptions/expectations and genetic drivers. You will also learn a lot about yourself as you learn about people, which will make you a more effective coach.

4. Coaching others right away.

You learn how to coach well by coaching others within the first six to eight months of entering our training programs. Because most of our students already have some experience in working with others, we suggest that you work with coachees just as soon as you master the core coaching essentials, competencies and tools. With time, training and experience, you'll become masterful. We believe that you'll never become masterful without practice, so you'd better dive right in! You'll get more out of your coach training if you are working with between 5 and 25 coachees.

5. Being coached yourself.

You learn how to coach well by being coached. Most coaches work with a CoachInc.com Professional Mentor Coach™ (PMC) as well as one or more buddy coaches. A Professional Mentor Coach is a coach who has a track record of mentoring new coaches. A buddy coach is a friend or colleague that you coach and who coaches you, for free. By having your own Professional Mentor Coach, as well as buddy coaches, you'll quickly discover what you like and don't like in each coach's style, which accelerates your own training process.

6. Learning by listening to masters.

You learn how to coach well by listening to the best coaches via TeleClass, RealAudio or audiotape. Listen to as many coaches as you possibly can, because the best way to learn advanced coaching techniques is to listen and observe.CoachInc.com has developed over 500 hours of audiotapes of masterful coaches. The real-time coaching tapes are organized by coachee type and situation, so you learn both different styles of coaching as well as how to coach specific types of coachees.

7. Tapping into the collective wisdom at CoachInc.com.

You learn how to coach well by referring to the written curriculum in our textbooks when you need help with a specific coachee or situation. Students are also encouraged to bring challenging coachee situations to the TeleClasses for discussions with others. Also CoachInc.com's Special Interest Groups are a place to tap into the combined wisdom of coaches with similar interests.

8. Participating in TeleClasses.

You learn how to coach well by participating in TeleClasses on virtually every aspect of coaching and every type of coachee. TeleClasses are led by Faculty members who are accredited, professional coaches trained through CoachInc.com. A TeleClass is a conference call, so all you need is a land-line telephone. You can call into your classes from anywhere in the world. Each TeleClass is conducted by a faculty member who discusses the key learning points of the class, and allows ample time to present case studies. A complete list of TeleClasses is located in Part Five.

9. Using coaching programs with coachees.

You learn how to coach well by learning programs that you can use immediately with coachees. There are times when you coach intuitively based on what your coachee needs during that coaching session, but there are times when the person being coached wants more structure and focus. For example, a coachee starting a new business usually wants help creating and implementing a plan, and also wants to make sure he or she isn't forgetting anything. The solution? The New Business Start Up Program. Or, for coachees who want to reduce stress, manage their time, enforce boundaries, and raise standards, use The Personal Foundation Program. CoachInc.com has developed many programs that you can use and share with individual coachees, with no royalty required.

10. Developing yourself.

You learn how to coach well by developing and evolving yourself along the way. The title of this book is "Becoming a Coach." It's not "Doing Coaching." Being a great coach is one part skill development and one part personal development. In other words, the more you develop yourself as you develop your skills and abilities, the more attractive you will be to the best coachees. Most coaches who enter training programs at CoachInc.com have already been developing themselves personally for some time, but at CoachInc.com, you will accelerate your progress and also leap into the process of Personal Evolution, which is the next stage of personal development.

Summing Up...

So, now you know how we train the finest life, career, business and corporate coaches in the world. If our approach suits you, we would love to have you join one of the programs at CoachInc.com depending on your needs and goals.

SECTION 9

What Are The Advantages Of Enrolling In Coach U Or Corporate Coach U?

As you've seen, this book describes the CoachInc.com approach to coaching and coach training. Many people looking for coach training want to know the unique advantages of our training programs. This section details those advantages, which are enjoyed by our students and graduates.

1. A comprehensive, inclusive approach.

Because there isn't a single approach that works for everyone, we use a variety of approaches, strategies and paths to success, so that you can offer a complete and customize your coaching to each individual coachee.

Coaches come from all backgrounds and have different cultural and style preferences. The CoachInc.com approach is sensitive to this cultural diversity and is also very illuminating as you learn how to effectively coach individuals from all walks of life and from every region in the world.

2. Just-in-time-learning convenience.

Coaches want to learn what they need when they need it. Our flexible approach to TeleClass scheduling, use of self-study materials and access to other resources and other coaches makes this possible.

3. A flexible professional path.

Some coaches want to coach full-time, other people want to coach part-time and yet others want to integrate sound coaching skills and strategies into their current jobs or businesses. Thanks to the flexibility of our training programs, you can use your coaching skills in any way you want.

4. Leading edge information and tools.

Innovation is very important to us at CoachInc.com – you wouldn't buy stale bread from the store -- don't buy stale information from a training program. We constantly add new content and upgrade current content to make sure it's still relevant in a changing world. Recently we launched brand new curricula that reflect the continual development and evolution of the coaching profession. Our materials are fresh, better, effective, learnable and teachable. Our materials, three textbooks published by John Wiley & Sons, were developed using a key learning increment model, whereby all pieces of the curriculum stand alone, but still connect with other pieces of the curriculum.

"Coach U's Advanced Coaching Program gave me the tools to dramatically change another person's life for the better in the span of a five minute conversation and has also been an incredible experience in my own life's journey."
- Alan (Avrohom) Goldberg, United States

5. Access to an international coaching community.

CoachInc.com hosts a variety of special interest groups, coaching chapters and other groups throughout the world, and this provides a powerful community for our students and graduates. In addition to being trained at CoachInc.com, you have over 9,000 coaches for mutual support and referrals. You have thousands of specialists you can turn to for help with a coachee, employee, friend or family member. And you have that many more people to connect with, benefit and learn from, and enjoy. Both professional and personal relationships result from this network. There have even been several marriages! Here's what members of our community would like to share with you:

"My life changed dramatically from the moment I got my own coach, who was also trained at CoachInc.com. The quality of training, the caliber of the faculty and the openhearted support are unmatched anywhere. It really is amazing."
- Nancy Boyd, United States

Summing Up...

As you have read, there are many advantages to enrolling in a coach training program at CoachInc.com. Key to your decision will be the people you want to learn with. There are a number of common qualities that our participants share:

They are bright.

CoachInc.com attracts the best and brightest, people who have the intellectual capacity to handle the study materials, the emotional intelligence to intuit powerfully and the personal presence to attract coachees.

They are eager to learn.

Those who choose CoachInc.com already know a lot about people and about life, but also realize that there is more to learn about coaching and are willing to invest in themselves and in their professional skill set.

They understand the opportunity.

Becoming a coach is a personal, professional and business opportunity. We consider this to be a personal opportunity because you will grow and evolve yourself as you become a coach. A professional opportunity, because you develop a skill set that is universally applicable in every field of endeavor. Finally, becoming a coach is a business opportunity, since coaching is a potentially lucrative career that can allow you to design a delightful lifestyle.

They know this is the right step for them.
Timing is everything, and the individuals who enter CoachInc.com know that this is the right time to invest in learning that will pay off over a lifetime.

They are willing to be our partners.
As you have read elsewhere in this book, CoachInc.com is special. On one hand, you are our customer and we strive to keep you satisfied by sharing with you all we have. On the other hand, we are all in this together, given the evolving nature of this profession and the craft of coaching. Therefore, we need your input, collaboration and support as well.

SECTION 10

Questions About Coaching Answered

Can I earn a living at this?

Yes, you can. It usually takes between six months and four years to create a full-time coaching practice. The more people you know, the faster you can build your practice. CoachInc.com offers many classes and marketing tools on finding and retaining coachees. Thousands of coaches have built successful practices; many of the same coaches who feared they couldn't. How much you earn depends on your marketing efforts, your area of specialty and the size and strength of your network. After several years of coaching, most coaches earn between $50,000 and $100,000. Some earn $250,000 and more.

Do coaches do anything other than coach individuals?

Yes, often they do group coaching, lead TeleClasses, conduct local workshops, make presentations and speeches, offer audiotapes and distribute e-newsletters. You can coach as much as you wish or offer extra services to your coachees locally or globally. Being a coach allows you to offer multiple services and products, without the typical limits of most professions.

What licensing is required to be a coach?

Currently, there are virtually no governmental licensing requirements in any state or country. However, in some U.S. states, a coach needs to register with the state if they present themselves as a career counselor. Students at CoachInc.com who are also ICF Members receive up-to-the minute updates on local registration or licensing requirements. It is now becoming more and more important to become an ICF Certified Coach since coachees and organizations are becoming more educated and are more likely to ask for your credentials.

Are there other coach training firms?

Yes, there are at least a dozen ICF accredited coaching companies, with more forming each year. Every firm offers a particular approach to coach training and coaching. It gets a little tricky to compare ourselves with other firms, but we can say that CoachInc.com's training programs are the most complete, comprehensive, multidisciplinary, innovative and flexible programs available today. We are also the most established, respected and largest worldwide coach training organization.

Can a person coach part-time?

Most coaches do, at least initially. If you already have a job, business or are freelancing, we suggest that you set aside one or two evenings a week to coach. As you attract more coachees, you'll feel more confident about making the transition to full-time coaching. There isn't a one-size-fits-all approach to setting up your practice.

How long would a coachee work with an independent coach?

Anywhere from three months to five years. As you become more skillful, you'll notice that your coachees stay with you longer. They'll continue getting better results because you're doing a terrific job. Also, as you become a stronger coach, you'll start attracting stronger, more compatible coachees, who stay with you longer.

When should I start working with coachees?

As soon as you wish. The more you coach – even for free – the more you'll benefit from your training. Most people begin using coaching skills within two weeks of starting one of our coach training programs; others wait six to eight months.

It's entirely up to you. However, you do NOT need to wait until you know it all. If you meet someone that you can help, offer to so do and let him or her know you're new at this.

"The key is to take coachees straight away. The courses make more sense when you are coaching and once you start you won't want to stop!"
– Gavin Ingham, United Kingdom

Can a dependency be created between coach and coachee?

If a coachee is really needy or emotionally dependent, he or she should see a counselor, not a coach. The coach is a collaborative partner and works with individuals who want to reach goals, not help resolve emotional issues. The coach is helping the coachee to create a better future – more success, less stress and a more rewarding life.

If I enter CoachInc.com, what can I expect?

You're entering a new field and we will do a number of things to support your success, including:

- Give you the training and information you need to coach well.
- Help you fill your practice, via the most extensive marketing courses available in coach training programs.
- Provide you with thousands of coaching tools.
- Connect you with other coaches and experts in the CoachInc.com communities.

"The Coach U Core Essentials Fast Track Program, through its sound structure and practical experience, has given me the confidence to launch my coaching practice. The Coach U textbooks have been valuable daily resources, in spreading the public message about coaching, and in strengthening my personal and practice skills. I am very pleased."
- Jeanette Isaacs-Young, Australia

Okay, what do you expect of students?

In order for this to work, you must have:

- A commitment to be the best possible coach, not just a good coach.
- A willingness to learn and grow, even in areas you think you already know well.
- A readiness to be a model for your coachees, instead of just being an expert.
- A desire to be our partner in furthering the coaching profession.

Who do you recommend NOT enter Coach U or Corporate Coach U?

We rarely advertise; current students and graduates refer most students. Usually, someone hears about our coach training programs and wants more information. They either read this book, visit our website at www.coachinc.com or take one of our free or low-cost TeleClasses. By then, most people know if coaching is right for them. Therefore, our programs are self-selecting – the right people are naturally attracted. However, we do ask people who are emotionally or financially stressed not to enter our programs until they are ready. Becoming a trained coach is an investment in a strong future, not a quick solution to current personal or professional problems. If you're not ready right now, working with a coach may speed your preparation process.

Will I need to hire my own coach to become a coach?

This is entirely up to you. The most successful coaches (those making $75,000-$250,000 year) hired a mentor coach in order to ramp up more quickly and continually evolve themselves. Currently, about 50% of our coaches-in-training work with what are called Professional Mentor Coaches™. Fees range from $100 (group coaching) to $400 (individual coaching) a month.

Are coaches specializing?

If so, what are the most popular specialties?

Yes, they are. There are at least 100 specialties a coach can focus on. These are listed in Part Five.

"As a Coach U Graduate I made mistakes by not listening to my coaches when they said "choosing a niche will bring added value through your experience, background and Coach U training". Once I "listened to my coaches" and specialized, my business has taken off. Listen to your coach! "
Ron Mudge United States

What kind of background does a person need to be an effective coach?

We are asked this question a lot. It's nice to have a degree (a majority of our students have), but that's not required. There are many bright and effective coaches working without a college degree. Socially, coaches come from every background, given coaching is cross-cultural. You don't need to be an expert in everything, but you should have a personal spark, some life experience and a huge willingness to learn the craft of coaching. Your coachees want YOU as their coach; they don't want a coaching service. Use the training at CoachInc.com to improve your personal and professional skill set.

How will I know if I'm successful?

There are three different types of success for a coach.

One type of success is measured by looking at the people they coach. How quickly and easily does the coachee reach his or her goals? How much does the coachee grow and evolve?

The second type of success in coaching is measured by how successful the coach's practice is. How many coachees does he/she have? How easy is it for him/her to attract coachees? Is he or she making enough money?

The third definition of success is how a professional increases his or her own skill set by adding coaching skills and competencies to his/her list of talents.

What is CoachInc.com's history?

Coach U started training coaches in 1988, with a group of 12 coaches. One of them was Sandy Vilas, who became the owner of Coach U in 1996. Coach U officially started the Coach Training Program™ in 1992, and in 1997, Corporate Coach U was created to provide business and corporate coaching skills to individuals, organizations and corporations. Corporate Coach U then released the Coaching Clinic Facilitators Licensing Program (CCLP)®, a four-day corporate coach training course. In 1999, Corporate Coach U developed a Coaching Services Division to provide companies with highly trained executive coaches for their management teams. In 1999, CoachInc.com was created to serve as the umbrella organization for Coach U and Corporate Coach U.

In 2001, Coach U developed the Core Essentials Program™, which allows individuals to gain coaching skills in a smaller time frame. Corporate Coach U followed shortly with their Business Coaching Essentials Program™, and in 2002, CoachInc.com redesigned our curricula based on over ten years of design and delivery of personal and corporate coach training. We launched a new website, www.coachinc.com, and created the International Coach Directory, www.findacoach.com, to highlight our students and graduates, and bring potential coachees and qualified coaches together.

In 2003, we introduced our Core Essentials Fast Track Programs™, aimed at individuals who want to learn basic coaching skills, coachee types and practice building strategies in one month.

In 2005, we reorganized our curriculum to provide one Core Essentials Program™ for all students (either in TeleClass or fast track format) to allow new students to learn basic coaching skills before needing to decide whether to enroll in Coach U or Corporate Coach U. After completing the Core Essentials program, students can choose either the Advanced Coaching Program or the Advanced Corporate Coaching Program.

In 2005, John Wiley and Sons published our new textbooks, The *Essential Coaching Tools*, The *Coach U Personal and Corporate Coach Training Handbook* and The *Coach U Personal Development Workbook and Guide* which help you begin a coaching practice with proven tools, and work on your own personal foundation.

Over the years we've continuously upgraded our student learning experience, added dozens of programs that coaches can use with coachees, produced 500 hours of audiotapes, 4000+ pages of reference materials, and coined such terms as Clean Sweep™, Personal Foundation™, Irresistible Attraction™, among others. We've developed a partnership with our students and graduates to produce world-class coaches through the finest coach training in the world.

Coaching, Coach U and Corporate Coach U certainly have received a lot of media attention in the past ten years. Why is that?

The emergence of an important new profession IS newsworthy. Over 500 media stories have appeared on coaching, Coach U and Corporate Coach U since 1996. When Newsweek magazine did a full-page article on coaching and Coach U, that opened the doors to coverage by USA Today, Donahue, the New York Times, the Times of London, CBS This Morning, NBC Nightly News, CNN's Impact, Inc., Better Homes & Garden, Shape, The Wall Street Journal, USA Today, the Daily Globe, and scores of metropolitan daily newspapers and news programs around the world. Thanks to the media's coverage, most people know what coaching is and don't ask if you coach Little League when you say you are a professional coach. We've come a long way from the earliest days when half of the conversation was just to explain what coaching is.

Do you ever hear people say that coaching sounds like their ideal profession and that they wish they had heard about CoachInc.com training earlier?

Yes, we hear this all the time. We rarely advertise and rely on word of mouth and media coverage to get the word out, so we apologize if we didn't make ourselves known earlier.

And, we frequently hear from new coaches that they considered this profession for about 3 years before enrolling. Of course, they try not to regret the "lost" time.

Why has coaching become so popular?

Coaching has become so popular (we estimate that there are 30,000 coaches worldwide) because there is consumer demand for it. There are many reasons for this. First, as more people become self-employed or start their own businesses, they want a coach's structure, support and wisdom to help them be successful. Second, people are becoming more creative, selfish (in a good sense) and excited about life. People want to do more, be more and get more, and a coach is seen as a partner in this process. Third, time has become even more valuable and people don't want to wait for anything. A coach can usually help a coachee get what they want faster.

Do people become independent coaches for a lifetime?

They can if they want. After several years as a coach, you can pretty much pick your coachees and set your own course. Some coaches will coach for the next 30 years and absolutely love it. Others will coach for a few years and then select another career – one that probably uses many of the skills and principles they learned and used as a coach. Others will stay in their current job or profession and use coaching technology to become more effective. Your path will be entirely up to you, and you likely will learn the next phase of your path when it comes upon you, rather than planning it years in advance.

Summing Up...

Coaching is an exciting field, attracting many of the best and brightest from a number of other fields. The results of people being coached speak for themselves and are causing the profession to grow more than heavy marketing ever could. We're happy to answer any questions you have about the industry we pioneered and continue to develop. Call us at 1-800-48COACH or email us at admissions@coachinc.com.

SECTION 11

More Information On Our Coach Training Programs

Can I speak with students and graduates of the program?

Yes. The best way is to call our admissions team at 1-800-48COACH. Each team member is a CoachInc.com student or graduate and can answer your questions or refer you to other students or graduates.

Do CoachInc.com coaches ever meet in person?

Yes, we offer periodic live trainings in the U.S. and major cities worldwide. And over one hundred CoachInc.com chapters meet monthly – students and graduates as well as people interested in becoming a coach are welcome at these meetings. You are most welcome to attend and meet coaches in your area. They are happy to welcome you and to answer your questions about coaching, coach training and our profession. Most meetings are informal and include a group discussion on a current theme or coaching topic. For a list of local and virtual coaching chapters, please visit www.coachuchapters.com.

There are also monthly Special Interest Group (SIG) meetings, held on teleconferencing bridges, that bring together coaches from around the world with similar interests or coaching niches. For a list of SIGs open to the public, visit our web site at www.coachinc.com, select Coach U and then select Special Interest Groups from the menu on the left side of the page.

Do I have to have a computer or be on the Internet in order to enter one of CoachInc.com's programs?

Yes. If you don't have a computer now but are planning to buy one within 30 days, you may still enroll in a

CoachInc.com program. We can even provide system recommendations if you like. You may select a Windows or Macintosh computer system, although most students use Windows systems. If you already have a computer and aren't yet on the Internet, our admissions team can get you started and even make ISP recommendations (an ISP is the company that provides you access to the Internet, like AOL, Earthlink, etc.). Some students start with little computer experience, but our supportive staff and TeleClass leaders get them up and running in no time.

Why do I have to be on the Internet in order join CoachInc.com?

Several reasons. One is that you will register for TeleClasses via our 24/7 automated web-based system. You'll also receive updates and special invitations and news, connect with other students and the faculty via e-mail, and view newly added materials with your web browser. Also, if you're planning to become a professional coach, most of your coachees will be on the Internet, so you'll need to be there as well. Within 60 days of being online, you'll recognize how essential it is to your professional and financial success.

Can I hire a Professional Mentor Coach™ instead of entering a coach training program?

You could, but you'd only be getting half the picture. A mentor coach is trained to help you make the most of the training provided at CoachInc.com, not to provide coach training. Only with our coach training programs can you learn (and be permitted to use) our hundreds of coaching skills, proprietary programs and marketing tools. Your Professional Mentor Coach™ is for you, but doesn't train you in the CoachInc.com technology.

Don't the phone calls to the TeleClasses get expensive?

Long distance costs continue to drop. Some services in North America offer long distance as low as 3 to 6 cents a minute, 24 hours a day. You may use any long distance carrier you wish, except those that operate using internet telephony and all cellular or mobile phone services. There are no special conference call charges. Many international students use competitively priced calling cards. Coaching is a worldwide phenomenon, and we're thrilled when coaches make the effort to call in for live classes from all over the world.

"I have made all my TeleClass calls from my home in Perth, in Western Australia...the most isolated city in the world! It took a little while to sort out phone plans and service providers but I have managed to cut my bill to 2/3 of the original cost -- now it costs no more to do a TeleClass than it would cost to pay for petrol and parking going to a university!"
– Kathryn Andrew, Australia

What happens during a typical TeleClass?

Most of the formal training you receive in our programs is done via conference call. Students call into a teleconferencing bridge for an hour or more, and work their way through one of the courses in the program over several weeks. TeleClasses meet anywhere from 4 to 12 consecutive weeks on the same day and time each week, and are conveniently scheduled throughout the day. A faculty member conducts each session. The faculty member covers the key learning points of the course and works with students to understand, integrate and learn the coaching concepts, skills or strategies of that course. Classes are interactive, much like a graduate-school discussion, and students may also engage in role-plays, peer coaching and case studies, depending on the course.

How do I actually learn via a TeleClass? How much homework should I expect?

On your TeleClasses, you learn by listening, experiencing, discussing and even role-playing, guided by an experienced faculty member. There is ample time for you to ask your leader or fellow students for help with handling a coachee situation or what to do more effectively. You can expect about an hour of homework for every hour of TeleClass, although this will vary by faculty member and by class.

Who are the faculty members at CoachInc.com? What are their backgrounds?

Faculty members are full-time coaches, so you will be learning from professionals who coach every day. Most faculty members lead about 10 hours of TeleClasses a month. The faculty members come from many different backgrounds, but they are all professional, experienced, personally evolved and excited about sharing what they know works with coachees. Our faculty members are experts in understanding what motivates, inspires, influences and develops them. Some of our faculty members are specialists, meaning that they work mainly with a single type of coachee, such as executives or those in career transition. The majority of our faculty are Professional Certified Coaches (PCCs) or Master Certified Coaches (MCC's) certified through the International Coach Federation (ICF).

How does one become a faculty member?

Every CoachInc.com graduate is eligible for training as a faculty member once they receive a Professional Certified Coach (PCC) or Master Certified Coach (MCC) designation with the ICF. Then, you can apply to the Faculty Training Program, where you'll learn the fundamentals of conducting interactive, evocative TeleClasses. By the end of the training, we will know if you're right for leading our TeleClasses.

I live outside North America. How is the program geared toward me?

Currently, there are CoachInc.com students and graduates in over 50 countries, and we are fully staffed in the United Kingdom/Europe as well as Australia/New Zealand. Most students are English-speaking. We have also developed partnerships with people and companies trained in using our materials in Italy, South Korea, Asia and Japan. For the most current contact information visit www.coachinc.com, and click on the 'Contact Us' button at the bottom left hand side of the screen or see Part Five.

And, it's important to note that there is reduced TeleClass availability for those residing in Australia and New Zealand during local evening hours.

Is certification available?

Yes. The Coach U Certified Graduate (CUCG) and the Corporate Coach U Certified Graduate (CCUCG) designations are available for graduates of our advanced training programs, after they meet a number of qualifications, including a minimum number of documented coaching hours; being coached/mentored by an approved mentor coach; having letters of recommendation; and, passing an interview.

In 2006, we will be offering a new certification for Core Essentials and Core Essentials Fast Track students – the Core Essentials Certified Graduation (CECG) designation.

There are many coaching designations offered in the coaching world, but none carry the cachet of a Coach U or Corporate Coach U certification, because none require the depth and breadth of training and competency demanded by our certification processes. These requirements make you eligible to apply to the International Coach Federation (ICF) for the designation of Associated Certified Coach (ACC), Professional Certified Coach (PCC), or Master Certified Coach (MCC).

What is the philosophical basis for the CoachInc.com approach to coaching?

That's a tricky question because we are a synthesis of at least a dozen disciplines and fields of study, including organizational development, leadership, entrepreneurship, personal development, sports, the healing arts, transformation, spirituality, philosophy and marketing. We use and teach concepts, strategies, principles, theories, practices, systems, models, and language from these fields in order to produce an integrated coaching technology. These are some of our beliefs:

On coaching
We believe that our job as coaches is to help people get what they most want in life. Everything a coach does with or for a coachee is oriented around that. We push for nothing but the coachee's true desires. And there is nothing more important than our coachee's satisfaction with our work.

On people
We believe that each person is unique and special and that we are all connected. As we strengthen ourselves, we strengthen everyone around us. We also feel that people are evolving, not just changing -- what it means to be human continues to evolve and unfold.

On life
We believe that life comes to us as a series of messages. If you see the message and respond to it, the message is an opportunity, but if you ignore or don't see the message, it becomes a problem. The better you can see and the faster

you respond, the more opportunities and fewer problems you will have.

What is the culture like at CoachInc.com?

CoachInc.com is a very unique place that fulfills a variety of roles. We are:

- A graduate-level school.
- Host to an international community of coaches.
- A dynamic research and development facility.
- A publisher and an electronic broadcast company.
- Professional home to over 9,000 coaches.

There is no other organization like CoachInc.com anywhere in the world. Everyone who enters our training program wants to become an effective and successful coach in the most current, practical and comprehensive manner. Most of them are well educated and already successful. In other words, they – and you – are the perfect partners for us. We share what we know works with our students, and you share what you know about life. We give you the tools you need to be a successful coach and you help us to create even better tools. It's a mutually beneficial, inter-developmental and cooperative relationship. It's a true partnership.

What is CoachInc.com's mission?

<u>CoachInc.com</u>

Vision: Everyone has a coach

Mission: To train the finest personal, business and corporate coaches worldwide.

Purpose: To develop the most extensive collection of tools for our coaches to use for the success of their coachees and their own practice.

Coach U

Vision: A world in which all people prosper and contribute in a meaningful manner.

Mission: To train the finest personal and business coaches in the world.

Purpose: To provide a compelling learning environment to master the skills of coaching.

Corporate Coach U

Vision: Corporate Coach U is the leading international provider of business and corporate coach training and services to individuals and organizations.

Mission: To develop professional corporate coaches and train Licensed Coaching Clinic Facilitators, who develop coaching skills and competencies for organizations.

Purpose: To provide a learning experience to master corporate coaching competencies, and provide coaching services that support specific organizational needs.

What are CoachInc.com's systems and structures?

Because CoachInc.com is a virtual organization, the delivery, customer service systems and state-of-the-art technologies we use are especially important. Briefly:

- We lease 45 teleconference bridges with a weekly capacity of 100,000 students.
- The International Coach Directory at www.findacoach.com has over 1700 coaches and receives 100,000 visitors annually.
- Students register for TeleClasses in real-time, via our website, with immediate confirmation.
- Our more than 30 staff and 120 faculty members deliver the training and operate the organization from many countries.

- Hundreds of volunteers develop the intellectual property, host Special Interest Groups and run the Coach U Chapters worldwide.

Summing Up...

One of the most interesting things about CoachInc.com is how we run the business, especially given the virtual nature of it. We value our students and know that our process works because our students and graduates tell us exactly that.

PART TWO

SECTION 1

Making It As An Independent Coach

How Does A Coach Find Coachees?

While many people who become coaches want to use coaching methods and skills in their current professions, many coaches develop a private practice. And of all the questions we answer each year from prospective coaches, we are most often asked, "How can I find coachees?"

Over the past 10 years, CoachInc.com has perfected the art of practice development and offers the most comprehensive practice development courses available in the industry. We also have an International Coach Directory, www.findacoach.com, which is the exclusive directory for CoachInc.com students and graduates. The International Coach Directory has brought hundreds of coaches and coachees together.

We suggest you focus on the proven, relationship-based methods to build your coaching practice. Here are just four of the 100 ways we've identified:

1. Expand your referral network.

From a marketing perspective, you are worth the value of your network, squared. In other words, if you have/know 100 people in your personal or professional network, your marketing value is $10,000 (100 x 100). We don't know if this equation is provable, but it illustrates the value of having as many people in your network as possible.

As a coach, you will benefit by expanding your personal and professional network. There are dozens of socially acceptable ways to build your network to a "critical mass." These techniques work even if you are not a gregarious person.

When you have enough people in your network, the phone rings with referrals. Wouldn't you rather respond to business coming to you than trying to push people to hire you as a coach? Two of the most effective ways to increase and strengthen your network are to use the Team 100 Checklist and the Jane Smart Letter.

The Team 100 Checklist™

We have developed a list of 100 professionals, such as attorneys, bankers, plumbers and the like. Using the checklist (there's a copy in Part Five), you will compile a list of everyone you know who fits into one of the professions listed on the form. Then, simply call each person to let him or her know what you do, who you do it for and how people benefit from your coaching services.

The Jane Smart Letter™

Petrified to pick up the phone? No problem. You can use what we call the Jane Smart letter (yes, Jane Smart is a hypothetical coach whose name we made up, but by now we like her so well, we think we'll keep referring to this sample marketing letter in this way). Basically, this is a letter of self-introduction that you can send, fax or email to the people in your address book. It's creatively and professionally worded to explain what coaching is and outline exactly what you do with coachees. The Jane Smart Letter works very well, because it is not a typical introductory or promotional letter. We've included one version of it in Part Five.

2. Coach for free if necessary.

Part of being a great coach is recognizing when people around you can benefit from your time, encouragement, advice or presence. One of the most successful strategies is something simple called generosity. In other words, when you see a need, you offer to help, whether you get paid for it or not.

If you already have a professional practice and a strong reputation in your current field, you may not need or want to be as generous as we're suggesting. But if you want more coachees, you may want to have some pro bono coachees. What we suggest is that you seek to serve instead of sell. It's a huge shift and leap of faith to take your focus off building your coaching revenue and instead concentrate on being generous with your time and resources.

It's fair to say that you already know at least 25 people who could benefit from your coaching. Not sure how to help these individuals you have earmarked? No problem -- just ask how you can help. They will tell you, and your coaching relationship will be off and running, without you having to sell yourself or coaching.

3. Start an e-newsletter.

One of the most successful ways to build a full practice is to start an electronic newsletter. Pick a topic that would appeal to your ideal coachees and start sending out your e-newsletter every week or two to people who want to subscribe to it. You can even make it a daily tip if you wish. Tens of millions of individuals on the Internet subscribe to these free e-newsletters. As you build your subscriber base, you'll find that about 1-5% of them will either become coachees, refer coachees to you or will take a TeleClass you offer. If you don't like the idea of selling your coaching services to people around you, then virtual marketing is your best bet because it attracts coachees to you.

4. Improving your life.

Can you get new coachees just by improving your own life? Yes! The happier you are with the quality of your own life, the better you'll feel about telling people that you are a coach. We recommend that coaches first start with the Clean Sweep Program™, which is included in Part Five. This is a 100-point checklist that will guide you through the life improvement process in 4 primary areas of your life: Relationships, Physical Environment, Money and Well-Being. As you increase your score on this checklist, you'll naturally attract coachees.

Summing Up...

Most new coaches are concerned about their ability to attract enough coachees to build a vibrant practice, so the four strategies above should provide some peace of mind. At CoachInc.com, we know that finding coachees is extremely important and we do more than any professional training school to give you every marketing tool and strategy to fill your practice.

PART THREE

SECTION 1

Finding A Coach

I am looking for a coach

CoachInc.com has created one of the industry's leading coach referral systems, www.findacoach.com, featuring personal and corporate coaches from around the world. Each coach listed is a student or graduate of CoachInc.com's coach training programs.

The site is designed to respond to each visitor's unique needs. Unlike most directories, FindACoach.com matches your needs with the coaches who will be best able to help you reach your goals. We do this in a unique environment that allows you to establish your own search parameters and how you wish to view your results. You can look for a coach based on parameters such as:

- Your goals
- A coach's background
- Specific geographical locations
- Languages and coaching delivery methods
- Coaching niches and areas of specialization
- Fee range
- Years of experience and education
- A coach's mission and vision
- Unique situations and challenges

All CoachInc.com coaches can list themselves on the directory with either a basic listing, or a full listing with five pages of detailed information about themselves, their practices, and how they can work with you to achieve your personal and business success. The site is completely confidential and it is up to you whether to contact and work with a coach. You can bookmark specific profiles, print out a listing of all the coaches you are interested in, or email them directly for more information.

Questions to ask a coach

Here are some questions that you might want to ask a coach during the interview stage. You can find the answers to some of these questions on the coach's website or in their profile at www.FindACoach.com.

- Who do you like to work with?
- Where were you trained?
- Have you graduated from your coach training program? If not, tell me about where you are at in the process.
- What certifications do you hold through your coach training program?
- What certifications do you hold through your professional coaching association, such as the International Coach Federation (ICF)?
- How long have you been coaching?
- What does working with a coachee typically look like?
- On average, how long does a coachee stay?
- What does your long-term vision of your practice look like?
- What are the areas of your experience and expertise?
- What initially attracted you to the coaching profession?
- How much do you charge?
- Which forms of payment do you accept?
- What can you tell me about yourself?
- Would you mind putting me in touch with a few current or past coachees to check your references?

Summing Up...

We invite you to explore our directory, www.FindACoach.com, to see the many ways that working with a coach can improve your quality of life.

PART FOUR

SECTION 1

Taking Action

Are you ready to enroll right now?

If you're ready to begin your coach training, you can register online at CoachInc.com by going to www.coachinc.com, clicking on either Coach U or Corporate Coach U, and selecting the Core Essentials Program. Then, click on the link at the end of the paragraph to find detailed information about the program and enroll. It's that easy.

Shortly after you enroll online, an Admissions Officer will contact you to complete the process. At this time, you may ask any questions that you have or express concerns, if any, as to whether you are indeed enrolling into the right program for your needs.

If you require assistance at any time or wish to discuss payment plans, please call 1-800-48-COACH or email admissions@coachinc.com.

1. A brief overview of CoachInc.com's programs

For more specific information about these programs, please visit our websites. We suggest you visit our websites regularly as we do post new programs and special events from time to time.

Coach Inc.com Introductory Programs:

- Becoming A Coach TeleClass – 4 Weeks
- Ask-The-Coach Q&A Session – 1 Hour

Coach Inc.com Programs Leading to ICF Certification:

- The TeleClass-based Core Essentials Program (CEP) or the equivalent live and in-person Core Essentials Fast Track program (CEFTP)

Coach U Program:

- Advanced Coaching Program Program (ACP)

Corporate Coach U Program:

- Advanced Corporate Coaching Program (ACCP)

Corporate Coach U's Program that meets eligibility requirements for ICF Coaching Continuing Education hours:

- Coaching Clinic Facilitators Licensing Program™ (CCLP)– In person

Experiencing CoachInc.com's products and services

If you would like to get to know us better, or to experience a TeleClass, we suggest you sign up for one or more of these TeleClasses.

1. The Ask-The-Coach Q&A TeleClass – complimentary one-hour session

Want to know more about the exciting and rapidly developing coaching field? Both Coach U and Corporate Coach U offer free informational sessions by telephone to anyone who has an interest in coaching. Here, you will interact with experienced faculty members and others who are interested in coaching and you'll learn more about the following:

- An overview of CoachInc.com's various training programs.
- Program costs for each program including payment plan information.
- How long it takes to complete the programs and what's involved in taking classes by teleconferencing.
- The certifications available to participants graduating from CoachInc.com as well as the International Coach Federation (ICF), the oldest,

most-recognized and largest professional coaching association.

- The importance of language and a replicable model for coaching.
- The advantages and ease of learning through the TeleClass format.
- How to take advantage of mentor coaching programs for new participants who want to accelerate their individual and professional development with the help of a Professional Mentor Coach™.
- How to register for a program and get started on your path to becoming a masterful coach.

Understandably, each organization's question and answer session will focus on the programs available within their own school, so you may want to enroll in both. You will leave the Q&A classes with your questions answered and you will know if one of CoachInc.com's training programs is right for you at this time. Also, by experiencing the TeleClass environment used in the Q&A, you'll be able to determine if this format suits your learning and communication styles.

2. The four-week "Becoming a Coach TeleClass"

This TeleClass is for anyone who is interested in coaching. All you need is a telephone to be part of this information-rich TeleClass, which is not only an informational resource, but also will give you an experience of virtual learning and training. During this four-week course, we will cover how to get started as a coach, the intersection between personal development and coaching, coaching models that you can start using today and business basics including marketing strategies.

Experiencing other products & services

- Coach Referral Service. Visit The International Coach Directory/Find A Coach Referral Service at www.findacoach.com if you are looking to work with a coach on a short- or long-term basis. This service will assist you in finding the right coach for you based on location or keyword searching.

- The Bookstore features general merchandise including coaching books and audiotapes. Visit any of our websites and click on "Coaching Well," then click on "The Book Store."
- The Assessment Center. Whether you're interested in learning more about Corporate Coach U's popular "Personal Communications Styles Inventory" or a number of other assessment instruments, visit any of our websites and click on "Coaching Well," then click on "The Assessment Center."
- Coaching On Demand. If you are looking for immediate coaching services, you might want to visit our Coaching On Demand site at www.coachingondemand.com. With this service, you can talk to a coach live for just-in-time coaching. You can also visit any of our websites and click on "Coaching Well," click on "Coach Referral" then click on "Coaching On Demand."

3. Making your choice

Here are some observations from coaches that have chosen to invest in a CoachInc.com coach training program:

"I investigated every coach training program that I could find and decided on Corporate Coach U because of their specific focus on Corporate Coaching. The team at CoachInc.com never pressured me to enroll and provided information in a professional manner. Having spent much of my career in sales, I appreciated it."
- Susan Cantwell, United States

"I rarely make quick decisions and studied Coach U and the coaching process for about 18 months before taking the plunge. I finally woke up one day saying, 'The time is now!' and enrolled that day. I am so glad I did...it is well worth the investment!"
– Marilyn Hall

"I wasn't sure about enrolling in Coach U at first, but it turned out to be one of the best choices I've ever made. Besides the outstanding curriculum, the Coach U community of coaches is a family and every student and graduate is made to feel a part of that family. If I never had a client, the personal growth and development I have received has been worth every penny and every minute. And I got a new 'extended family' in the package."
– Judy Irving, PCC, United States

4. Make the decision today

You could wait to make the decision to start, but why?

- Call us at 1-800-48COACH
- Email us at admissions@coachinc.com
- Visit our websites at:
  - CoachInc.com – www.coachinc.com
  - Coach U – www.coachu.com
  - Corporate Coach U – www.ccui.com

PART FIVE

SECTION 1

The Team 100 Checklist

Helping clients and coachees get the results they need requires a team effort by a Coach and other professionals. The Team 100 Checklist™ works like a contact database or online address book: you select 100 professionals who you want on your team. With the right players, here's what can happen:

- Your coachees have access to a strong network.
- You can tap into high-expertise immediately.
- Most problems or needs can be solved, fast.
- Referrals start flowing among team members

How to Play:

1. Decide to get a full team within 1 year.
2. Fill in the team members you now know.
3. Start networking to fill in the other slots.
4. Pass around blank forms to associates.
5. Get yourself on other people's Team 100™ lists.

Give yourself credit as you get points from the 100-point program. Fill in columns from the bottom up.

A. Biz & Work

Running a business, managing a career, finding work that you enjoy all come easier when you have experts and models to guide and inspire you.

New Business Specialist
    Name:____
    Contact Info:__________________________________
Career Consultant/Planner
    Name:____
    Contact Info:__________________________________

Graphic Artist
Name:______________________________________
Contact Info:________________________________

Printer/Copy Place
Name:______________________________________
Contact Info:________________________________

Turnaround Business Expert
Name:______________________________________
Contact Info:________________________________

Corporate Trainer
Name:______________________________________
Contact Info:________________________________

Professional Networker
Name:______________________________________
Contact Info:________________________________

Internet Marketing Expert
Name:______________________________________
Contact Info:________________________________

Web Presence Provider
Name:______________________________________
Contact Info:________________________________

Personal Marketer
Name:______________________________________
Contact Info:________________________________

Business Coach
Name:______________________________________
Contact Info:________________________________

Corporate Coach
Name:______________________________________
Contact Info:________________________________

Executive Coach
Name:______________________________________
Contact Info:________________________________

Business Diagnostic Coach
Name:______________________________________
Contact Info:________________________________

Marketing Coach
Name:______________________________________
Contact Info:________________________________

Professional Writer
Name:______________________________________
Contact Info:________________________________

Computer Consultant
Name:______________________________________
Contact Info:________________________________

Hard Disk Crash Recovery Specialist
Name:____________________________________
Contact Info:_______________________________
Software Consultant
Name:____________________________________
Contact Info:_______________________________
Headhunter
Name:____________________________________
Contact Info:_______________________________

___ Number of items checked (20 max)

B. Money & Legal

The only thing in the way of your financial independence is great advice and the willingness to apply it.

Small Business Attorney
Name:____________________________________
Contact Info:_______________________________
Real Estate Attorney
Name:____________________________________
Contact Info:_______________________________
Tax Attorney
Name:____________________________________
Contact Info:_______________________________
International Attorney
Name:____________________________________
Contact Info:_______________________________
Estate Attorney
Name:____________________________________
Contact Info:_______________________________
Copyright/Trademark Attorney
Name:____________________________________
Contact Info:_______________________________
Criminal Attorney
Name:____________________________________
Contact Info:_______________________________
Financial Planner
Name:____________________________________
Contact Info:_______________________________
Banker
Name:____________________________________
Contact Info:_______________________________

Realtor
Name:____________________________________
Contact Info:______________________________
Venture Capitalist
Name:____________________________________
Contact Info:______________________________
Stockbroker
Name:____________________________________
Contact Info:______________________________
CPA
Name:____________________________________
Contact Info:______________________________
Insurance - Life/Health/Disability
Name:____________________________________
Contact Info:______________________________
Insurance - Liability
Name:____________________________________
Contact Info:______________________________
Insurance - Home/Auto
Name:____________________________________
Contact Info:______________________________
Bookkeeper/Bill Paying Service
Name:____________________________________
Contact Info:______________________________
Grant Writer
Name:____________________________________
Contact Info:______________________________
Property Manager
Name:____________________________________
Contact Info:______________________________
Money Manager
Name:____________________________________
Contact Info:______________________________

___ Number of items checked (20 max)

C. Personal & Health
Our bodies, minds and spirits can benefit from these experts.

MD - Internist
Name:____________________________________
Contact Info:______________________________

MD - Ophthalmologist
Name:____
Contact Info:__________________________________
MD - Cosmetic Surgeon
Name:____
Contact Info:__________________________________
MD - Dermatologist
Name:____
Contact Info:__________________________________
MD - Sports
Name:____
Contact Info:__________________________________
MD - Psychiatrist
Name:____
Contact Info:__________________________________
Nutritionist
Name:____
Contact Info:__________________________________
ND (Naturopath)
Name:____
Contact Info:__________________________________
Massage Therapist
Name:____
Contact Info:__________________________________
Chiropractor
Name:____
Contact Info:__________________________________
Pharmacist
Name:____
Contact Info:__________________________________
Movement Therapist
Name:____
Contact Info:__________________________________
Acupuncturist
Name:____
Contact Info:__________________________________
Diagnostician
Name:____
Contact Info:__________________________________
Therapist - Depression
Name:____
Contact Info:__________________________________
Therapist - ADD Expert
Name:____
Contact Info:__________________________________

Therapist - Relationships
Name:____________________
Contact Info:____________________
Fertility Expert
Name:____________________
Contact Info:____________________
Dentist/Cosmetic Dentist
Name:____________________
Contact Info:____________________
Speech Therapist
Name:____________________
Contact Info:____________________

___ Number of items checked (20 max)

D. Personal Services
These are services that make our lives easier.

Housekeeping/Cleaning
Name:____________________
Contact Info:____________________
Travel Agent
Name:____________________
Contact Info:____________________
Event Planner
Name:____________________
Contact Info:____________________
Florist
Name:____________________
Contact Info:____________________
Professional Gift Service
Name:____________________
Contact Info:____________________
Portrait Photographer
Name:____________________
Contact Info:____________________
Caterer
Name:____________________
Contact Info:____________________
Seamstress/Tailor
Name:____________________
Contact Info:____________________
Childcare/Babysitter
Name:____________________
Contact Info:____________________

Minister/Clergy
Name:____
Contact Info:___________________________________
Auto Mechanic/Car Care
Name:____
Contact Info:___________________________________
Electrician
Name:____
Contact Info:___________________________________
Air Conditioning/Heating
Name:____
Contact Info:___________________________________
Plumber
Name:____
Contact Info:___________________________________
Professional Organizers
Name:____
Contact Info:___________________________________
Personal Concierge/Errands
Name:____
Contact Info:___________________________________
Dog Walker/Pet Sitter
Name:____
Contact Info:___________________________________
Good Book Maven
Name:____
Contact Info:___________________________________
Interior Designer/Decorator
Name:____
Contact Info:___________________________________
Handyman/woman
Name:____
Contact Info:___________________________________

___ Number of items checked (20 max)

E. Extreme Self Care

Extreme self-care refers to the practice of taking exceptionally good care of your body, mind and spirit. The professionals below can make a big difference in your emotional, physical and energy levels.

Skin Care Specialist/Spa
Name:____
Contact Info:___________________________________

Personal Assistant (Real)
Name:_______________
Contact Info:_______________
Personal Assistant (Virtual)
Name:_______________
Contact Info:_______________
Personal Trainer
Name:_______________
Contact Info:_______________
Healthy Food Delivery
Name:_______________
Contact Info:_______________
Personal Coach
Name:_______________
Contact Info:_______________
Spiritual Advisor/Clergy
Name:_______________
Contact Info:_______________
Manicurist/Pedicurist
Name:_______________
Contact Info:_______________
Jeweler
Name:_______________
Contact Info:_______________
Certified Rolfer
Name:_______________
Contact Info:_______________
Image/Color Consultant
Name:_______________
Contact Info:_______________
Personal Makeover Coach
Name:_______________
Contact Info:_______________
Communication Coach
Name:_______________
Contact Info:_______________
Feng Shui Consultant
Name:_______________
Contact Info:_______________
Reiki Master
Name:_______________
Contact Info:_______________
Alexander Technique Expert
Name:_______________
Contact Info:_______________

Irresistible Attraction Coach
Name:____
Contact Info:__________________________________
Visual Artist Consultant
Name:____
Contact Info:__________________________________
Lifestyle Design Coach
Name:____
Contact Info:__________________________________
Psychic
Name:____
Contact Info:__________________________________

___ Number of items checked (20 max)

Additional Team Member Ideas:

Elder Care specialist, Self-Defense Trainer, Dental Insurance, Pest Control, Retirement Planner, Home School Expert, Vet, Carpet Cleaner, Painter, Funeral Director, Decorator, Landscaper, Pediatrician, Architect, Optometrist, Grief Counselor, Strategic Planner, Pet Trainer, Holistic Medical Practitioner, Spiritual Healer, Development Disabilities, Personal Shopper, International Law Expert, Inter-Cultural Communicator (Diversity Trainer), International Travel Expert, Translator, Interpreter, Foreign Language Teacher, International Conference Coordinator.

Intellectual Property Notice:

CoachInc.com
P.O. Box 881595, Steamboat Springs, CO 80488-1595
1-800-48COACH • 1-800-FAX5655
admissions@coachinc.com
http://www.coachinc.com

SECTION 2

The Jane Smart Letter

The following Jane Smart letter (or your version of it) may be sent to friends, associates, and colleagues as well as members of your Team 100.

Dear Colleague:

Hello. You are one of 100 friends, associates and colleagues to whom I am sending this letter. I am expanding my practice to include coaching and I wanted to let you know the types of coachees I can do good work for and to ask you to be my partner in the development of my coaching practice. I have enclosed some material on the nature of coaching, but briefly, as a coach, I:

1. Help my coachees set larger, better, more rewarding personal and professional goals.
2. Speak with each coachee at least weekly to help him or her strategize and take action.
3. Ask more of my coachees than they – or others – might ask of themselves. The roles of the coach include: Advocate, Champion, Partner, Cheerleader and Sounding Board.

As you know, I have been a business management consultant for 11 years. By adding this coaching service and weaving in the coaching success principles, structures and technology, I can do far more for my coachees than before.

I am currently working with six coachees and my practice goal is to be working with 36 coachees. I do not advertise, but rely instead on my current coachees and my colleagues, like you, for referrals.

My specialty is working with the following types of coachees:

1. The Entrepreneur who is ready to at least double his or her business, quickly.
2. The Consultant who wishes to expand his/her practice significantly.
3. The CEO or Executive who needs to bring his or her organization to the next level.

I charge $350 per month for a weekly session. Coachees out of the area may use my toll-free coaching phone number.

Will you help? I am asking that you keep me in mind when you run across anyone who is one of the three types listed above. Also, if you know someone who you think would benefit from coaching – perhaps even yourself – I am happy to spend 30 minutes with them to see if I can help or by putting them in touch with one of my coaching colleagues who I think can do a great job for them. (There are over 9,000 coaches in my network and I am in touch with 150 of these who are part of a training program offered through CoachInc.com.)

I have enclosed several business cards. Please share these, or even ask me to call someone who has expressed an interest. Please keep in mind that from time to time my coachees will need the type of expertise that you provide and I would be honored to refer them to you.

Warmest regards,
Jane Smart, Coach

SECTION 3

The Clean Sweep Program

You have more natural energy when you are clear with your environment, health and emotional balance, money and relationships.

The Clean Sweep Program, developed by the staff, trainers and participants of Coach U, Inc., consists of 100 items which, when completed, give you the vitality and strength you want.

The program can be completed in less than one year.

Give yourself credit as you get points from the 100-point program. Fill in columns from the bottom up. Instructions for this assessment are on the last page.

# true items	Physical Environment	Health & Emotional Balance	Money	Relationships
1				
2				
3				
4				
5				
6				
7				
8				
9				
10				
11				
12				
13				
14				
15				
16				
17				
18				
19				
20				

PHYSICAL ENVIRONMENT

- o My personal files, papers and receipts are neatly filed away.
- o My car is in excellent condition (doesn't need mechanical work, repairs, cleaning or replacing)
- o My home is neat and clean. (vacuumed, closets clean, desks and tables clear, furniture in good repair; windows clean)
- o My appliances, machinery and equipment work well. (refrigerator, toaster, snow-blower, water heater, toys)
- o My clothes are all pressed, clean and make me look great. (no wrinkles, baskets of laundry, torn, out-of-date or ill-fitting clothes)
- o My plants and animals are healthy. (fed, watered, getting light and love)
- o My bed/bedroom lets me have the best sleep possible (firm bed, light, air.)
- o I live in a home/apartment that I love.
- o I surround myself with beautiful things.
- o I live in the geographic area I choose.
- o There is ample and healthy light around me.
- o I consistently have adequate time, space and freedom in my life.
- o I am not damaged by my environment.
- o I am not tolerating anything about my home or work environment.
- o My work environment is productive and inspiring. (synergistic, ample tools and resources; no undue pressure)
- o I recycle.
- o I use non ozone-depleting products.
- o My hair is the way I want it.
- o I surround myself with music that makes my life more enjoyable.
- o My bed is made daily.
- o I don't injure myself, or bump into things.
- o People feel comfortable in my home.
- o I drink purified water.
- o I have nothing around the house or in storage that I do not need.
- o I am consistently early or easily on time.

____ Number of checked items (25 max)

HEALTH & EMOTIONAL BALANCE

- I rarely use caffeine, including chocolate, coffee, tea, and cola. (less than 3 times per week, total)
- I rarely eat sugar. (less than 3 times per week, total)
- I rarely watch television. (less than 5 hours per week)
- I rarely drink alcohol. (less than 2 drinks per week)
- My teeth and gums are healthy. (have seen dentist in last 6 months)
- My cholesterol count is healthful.
- My blood pressure is healthful.
- I have had a complete physical exam in the past 3 years.
- I do not smoke tobacco or other substances.
- I do not use illegal drugs or misuse prescribed medications.
- I have had a complete eye exam within the past two years. (glaucoma check, vision test)
- My weight is within my ideal range.
- My nails are healthy and attractive.
- I don't rush or use adrenaline to get the job done.
- I have a rewarding life beyond my work or profession.
- I have something to look forward to virtually every day.
- I have no habits that I find to be unacceptable.
- I am aware of the physical or emotional problems or conditions I have, and I am now fully taking care of all of them.
- I consistently take evenings, weekends and holidays off and take at least two weeks of vacation each year.
- I have been tested for the AIDS antibody.
- I use well-made sunglasses.
- I do not suffer.
- I floss daily.
- I walk or exercise at least three times per week.
- I hear well.

____ Number of checked items (25 max)

MONEY

- o I currently save at least 10% of my income.
- o I pay my bills on time, virtually always.
- o My income source/revenue base is stable and predictable.
- o I know how much I must have to be minimally financially independent and I have a plan to get there.
- o I have returned or made-good-on any money I borrowed.
- o I have written agreements and am current with payments to individuals or companies to whom I owe money.
- o I have 6 months' living expenses in a money market-type account.
- o I live on a weekly budget that allows me to save and not suffer.
- o All my tax returns have been filed and all my taxes have been paid.
- o I currently live well, within my means.
- o I have excellent medical insurance.
- o My assets (car, home, possessions, treasures) are well insured.
- o I have a financial plan for the next year.
- o I have no legal clouds hanging over me.
- o My will is up-to-date and accurate.
- o Any parking tickets, alimony or child support are paid and current.
- o My investments do not keep me awake at night.
- o I know how much I am worth.
- o I am on a career/professional/business track that is or will soon be financially and personally rewarding.
- o My earnings are commensurate with the effort I put into my job.
- o I have no "loose ends" at work.
- o I am in relationship with people who can assist in my career/professional development.
- o I rarely miss work due to illness.
- o I am putting aside enough money each month to reach financial independence.
- o My earnings outpace inflation, consistently.

____ Number of checked items (25 max)

RELATIONSHIPS

- I have told my parents, in the last 3 months, that I love them.
- I get along well with my sibling(s).
- I get along well with my co-workers/coachees.
- I get along well with my manager/staff.
- There is no one who I would dread or feel uncomfortable "running across" (in the street, at an airport or party).
- I put people first and results second.
- I have let go of the relationships that drag me down or damage me. ("Let go" means to end, walk away from, state, handle, and no longer be attached to.)
- I have communicated or attempted to communicate with everyone who I have damaged, injured or seriously disturbed, even if it wasn't fully my fault.
- I do not gossip or talk about others.
- I have a circle of friends/family who love and appreciate me for who I am, more than just what I do for them.
- I tell people how they can satisfy me.
- I am fully caught up with letters and calls.
- I always tell the truth, no matter what.
- I receive enough love from people around me to feel good.
- I have fully forgiven those people who have hurt/damaged me, deliberate or not.
- I am a person of his/her word; people can count on me.
- I quickly clear miscommunications and misunderstandings when they do occur.
- I live life on my terms, not by the rules or preferences of others.
- There is nothing unresolved with past loves or spouses.
- I am in tune with my wants and needs and get them taken care of.
- I do not judge or criticize others.
- I do not "take personally" the things that people say to me.
- I have a best friend or soul-mate.
- I state requirements rather than complain.
- I spend time with people who don't try to change me.

____ Number of checked items (25 max)

Instructions

There are 4 steps to completing the Clean Sweep™ Program.

Step 1
Answer each question. If true, check the box. Be rigorous; be a hard grader. If the statement is sometimes or usually true please DO NOT check the box until the statement is virtually always true for you. (No "credit" until it is really true!) If the statement does not apply to you, or will never be true for you, check the box. (You get "credit" for it because it does not apply or will never happen.) And, you may change any statement to fit your situation better.

Step 2
Summarize each section. Add up the number of True boxes for each of the 4 sections and write those amounts where indicated. Then add up all four sections and write the current total in the box on the front of this form.

Step 3
Color in the Progress Chart on the front page. Always start from the bottom up. The goal is to have the entire chart filled in. In the meantime, you will have a current picture of how you are doing in each of the four areas.

Step 4
Keep playing until all boxes are filled in. You can do it! This process may take 30 or 360 days, but you can achieve a Clean Sweep! Use your coach or a friend to assist you. And check back once a year for maintenance.

Benefits
On the lines below, jot down specific benefits, results and shifts that happened in your life because you handled an item in the Clean Sweep Program.

Date	Benefit
_____	______________________________
_____	______________________________
_____	______________________________
_____	______________________________
_____	______________________________
_____	______________________________

Fill in the bar chart on the front panel as you increase your Clean Sweep scores.

CoachInc.com
P.O. Box 881595, Steamboat Springs, CO 80488-1595
1-800-48COACH • 1-800-FAX5655
admissions@coachinc.com
http://www.coachinc.com

SECTION 4

Self-Knowledge Score Sheet

SELF-KNOWLEDGE SCORE SHEET Knowing who you are contributes to higher levels of success	
5-Always *4-Frequently* *3-Usually* *2-Seldom* *1-Never*	The basis for success as a Coach is "being" who you are. Such understanding helps you select the vision and establish goals that are appropriate for you, your team and/or your company. You want to know your strengths, gifts, skills, competencies, limitations, even your wants and needs long before goals are established. Your values and principles will serve as guidance for your direction.
1 2 3 4 5	1. I know what my strengths and gifts are and exemplify them in all that I do.
1 2 3 4 5	2. I know what my Guiding Principles are and live by them every day.
1 2 3 4 5	3. I have a very high level of self-esteem and feel very good about myself.
1 2 3 4 5	4. I have explored my tolerations and have none in my life that I can do something about.
1 2 3 4 5	5. I respond in a proactive versus reactive ways.
1 2 3 4 5	6. I know what I want in life and have written my personal mission statement.
1 2 3 4 5	7. I have a positive attitude about life, people and situations.
1 2 3 4 5	8. I have established quality daily habits and am constantly raising my standards.
1 2 3 4 5	9. I have a great respect for differences and diversities.
1 2 3 4 5	10. I embrace the fact that disagreement is positive and out of disagreement comes new learning.
1 2 3 4 5	11. I have identified my needs and am responsible for satisfying them myself.
1 2 3 4 5	12. I am a self-appreciator and am able to appreciate others as well.
1 2 3 4 5	13. I admit when I make mistakes and learn from making them.
1 2 3 4 5	14. I tell the truth and speak my own truth as well as what I see as truth for others even when it seems risky to do so.
1 2 3 4 5	15. I am curious and practice discovery of possibilities.
1 2 3 4 5	16. I expect change to be the constant in my live and can adapt and cope as necessary. I am a change agent.
1 2 3 4 5	17. I am a lifelong learner and never miss an opportunity to expand my knowledge.
1 2 3 4 5	18. I am able to set my own ego aside so that I can connect with my heart.
1 2 3 4 5	19. I am action oriented and have a good level of proactivity. I follow through and get things done.
1 2 3 4 5	20. I take risks easily and can be fairly gutsy.

SECTION 5

Personal Presence Score Sheet

PERSONAL PRESENCE SCORE SHEET What your public demeanor teaches others about you	
5-Always *4-Frequently* *3-Usually* *2-Seldom* *1-Never*	Presence describes a person's bearing, especially when it commands respectful attention. Professional success as a Coach requires more than your coaching abilities. It requires personal/professional presence. Presence draws trust and relationships from others.
1 2 3 4 5	1. I am aware of the "first impressions" that I make.
1 2 3 4 5	2. I have identified my "real" style and "come from" that style publicly and privately.
1 2 3 4 5	3. I live a conscious life and am aware of all things around me.
1 2 3 4 5	4. I exude energy that is inviting to others because of its genuineness.
1 2 3 4 5	5. I remember people's names and connect because I am truly interested in them.
1 2 3 4 5	6. I am approachable. I maintain a relaxed readiness with head held high.
1 2 3 4 5	7. I am proud of myself and feel confident in my accomplishments.
1 2 3 4 5	8. I smile confidently, shake hands, and make eye contact..
1 2 3 4 5	9. I connect with others and have developed a broad network.
1 2 3 4 5	10. I ask questions of others that invite them to participate in conversation with me.
1 2 3 4 5	11. I watch for social cues from those around me.
1 2 3 4 5	12. I use both speech and silence as effective ways to communicate.
1 2 3 4 5	13. I think before I speak formulating my ideas succinctly.
1 2 3 4 5	14. I give and receive positive and constructive feedback with ease.
1 2 3 4 5	15. I am a very good storyteller and use stories to communicate and connect effectively.
1 2 3 4 5	16. I am humorous and like to lighten up situations whenever appropriate.
1 2 3 4 5	17. I am publicly modest. I take credit when deserved and share credit more than deserved.
1 2 3 4 5	18. I am able to set my own ego aside so that I can connect with my heart.
1 2 3 4 5	19. I am well read and am comfortable in conversations about what is going on in business and the world.
1 2 3 4 5	20. I enjoy people and people enjoy me.

SECTION 6

Coaching Specialties

As the demand for coaching grows, so too does the demand for coaching specialties. Below is a list of 101 Coaching Specialties, many of which have already become popular. Whether you are a coach in training wondering about different specialties or you are a coachee seeking a specialist, the following list should be very useful.
Note: Some specialties require special licensing/testing, or advanced training, qualifications and testing. Finally, some specialties are just now being popularized.

1. Corporate

- Corporate Coach
- Executive/CEO Coach
- Organizational Development Coach
- Management Coach
- Culture/Paradigm Shift Coach
- Leadership Coach
- Board of Directors' Coach
- Human Resource Coach
- Quality/TQM Coach
- Staff/Employee Coach

2. Marketing/Sales

- Sales Coach
- Public Relations Coach
- Marketing Coach
- Brand Management Coach
- Promotions Coach
- Pricing Strategy Coach
- Buzz-Development Coach
- Advertising Coach
- Direct Marketing Coach
- Personal Marketing Coach

3. Small Business

- New Business Coach
- Entrepreneur Coach
- Business Turnaround Coach
- MLM/Network Marketing Coach
- Networking Coach
- Budgeting/Planning Coach
- Business Financial Coach
- Mission Development Coach
- Marketing Coach
- Partner's Coach

4. Relationships

- Marriage Coach
- Family Coach
- Romance Coach
- Team Coach
- Parent Coach
- Love Coach
- Divorce Recovery Coach
- Couples' Coach
- Network Development Coach
- Intimacy Coach

5. Lifestyle

- Fresh Start Coach
- Generation X Coach
- Baby Boomer Coach
- Retirement Coach
- Lifestyle Design Coach
- Teen Coach
- Students' Coach
- Workaholics' Coach
- Transition Coach
- Personal Turnaround Coach

6. Quality of Life

- Nutrition/Diet Coach
- Exercise /Fitness Coach
- Vegan/Vegetarian Coach
- Recreation Coach
- Travel/Adventure Coach
- Wellness Coach
- Energy/Reiki Coach
- Makeover Coach
- Buff /Style Coach
- Stress Reduction Coach

7. Success Coach

- Motivation/Edge Coach
- Goals/Results Coach
- Idea/Creativity Coach
- Problem-solving/Solution Coach
- Time Management/Leverage Coach
- Strategic Coach
- Attraction/OS Coach
- Financial/Money Coach
- Career Coach
- Legacy/Achievement Coach

8. Special Markets

- Consultants/Coaches' Coach
- MDs/Health Professional/Dental Coach
- Attorney/Law Firm Coach
- CPA/Financial Service Professional Coach
- Trainers/Speakers' Coach
- Gay/Lesbian Coach
- Single Parents' Coach
- Realtors/Real Estate Coach
- Therapists/Counselors' Coach
- Ministers/Caregivers Coach

9. Personal Development

- Personal Foundation Coach
- Integrity Coach
- Balance Coach
- Co-dependency Coach
- Fear Coach
- Post-12-step Coach
- Resolution Coach
- Attainments Coach
- Spiritual Coach
- 12-step/Recovery/Addiction Coach

10. Special Skills & Situations

- Communication Coach
- Cyber Coach
- Internet/Web Coach
- Diagnostic Coach
- Futurist Coach
- Language/Phrasing Coach
- Learning Coach
- Software/Computer Coach
- Writing Coach
- Personal Organization Coach

And...

- General Practitioner Coach

SECTION 7

Core Essentials Program Courses

CE-101 CoachInc.com 101
This overview provides new students with the policies and procedures that support the student experience at CoachInc.com. This class is only for new students.
Number of class sessions: 1
Prerequisites: This course is a prerequisite for all other classes.

CE-110 New Coach Orientation
In this module, you will gain an understanding of the coaching profession and help you develop your own personal definition. You will gain knowledge of the coaching core competencies identified by the International Coach Federation (ICF), the steps needed to develop your coachees and providing continued structure for their growth and the Coaching Ethics for Internal and External Coaches.
Number of class sessions: 4
Prerequisites: CE-101 CoachInc.com 101

CE-120 Guiding Principles
In this module, you will gain an understanding of the Guiding Principles of Human Interaction which represent how people fundamentally interact, and which coaches generally accept as true. You will recognize the existence of these principles in everyone's life, whether in a personal or organizational setting.
Number of class sessions: 4
Prerequisites: CE-101 CoachInc.com 101

CE-130 Context for Coaching
In this module, you will learn how to effectively craft a coaching relationship to connect strongly with your coachee. You will be able to clearly distinguish between coaching and other professions, become familiar with the coaching framework and learn several coaching models.
Number of class sessions: 4
Prerequisites: CE-101 CoachInc.com 101

CE-210 Listening
In this module, you will learn how to effectively listen to your coachees. You will be able use the various listening skills to know what to listen for, avoid listening pitfalls and use the most appropriate skill at different points in a coaching conversation. You will be able to move freely and easily between the different types and focuses of listening and also to listen for clues that indicate where a person is on his or her path of development, and whether his or her issues are best referred to another type of professional.
Number of class sessions: 4
Prerequisites: All 100 series courses.

CE-212 Language
In this module, you will learn to identify your and your coachee's preferred language and continually choose the language that best conveys meaning, inspires, challenges or clarifiies. You will become aware of how your coachees use language to explain, defend, inform, describe and ask for what they want, need and value. By learning about the forms and uses of language, you will enhance your ability to express yourself and help others to do the same.
Number of class sessions: 4
Prerequisites: All 100 Series courses.

CE-214 Questioning
Powerful questioning is at the core of effective coaching. In this module, you will learn to craft and deliver great coaching questions. You will understand how the type, timing and impact of a coach's questioning differs from how questions show up in most conversations, and also how you can direct the flow of the coaching interaction for optimal benefit for the coachee.
Number of class sessions: 4
Prerequisites: All 100 series courses.

CE-216 Strategizing
Strategizing is a comprehensive coaching skill. In this module you will learn the tools to help your coachees develop effective strategies to accomplish their goals. This module will help you understand the framework of strategizing, as well as practical tools and information about how to become an effective strategist.
Number of class sessions: 4
Prerequisites: All 100 series courses.

CE-218 Messaging
In this module, you will learn what to say and how to say it, so that your messaging is effective and valuable to the coachee. Messaging is a powerful coaching tool that opens the possibility for a shift to occur. You will become familiar with the mechanics of messaging, including the two main methods used in coaching interactions, as well as the limitations and pitfalls of each.
Number of class sessions: 4
Prerequisites: All 100 series course.

CE-220 Acknowledging
In this module, you will learn how to effectively use acknowledgement to help your coachees achieve their vision. You will understand the framework of acknowledging, including the methods and stages, and even the perils and receive practical tools and information about skills, discernment of, and attitudes regarding acknowledging.
Number of class sessions: 4
Prerequisites: All 100 series course.

CE-225 Core Skills Practice Lab
Each participant has 20 minutes to coach, be coached and write a case study on an observed coaching session. Coach-the-coach occurs by faculty; feedback focuses on the development of the core coaching skills. Each participant must coach, be coached and write a case study to receive credit for this course.
Number of students: 16
Number of class sessions: 8
Prerequisites: All 100 and 200 series courses.

CE-310 Situational Coaching
In this module you will gain a basic understanding of common personal or professional conditions that a coachee experiences. While coaching cannot be done based on a single formula or recipe, it is possible for a coach to identify various types of coachees to create a framework from which to develop a coaching plan.
Number of class sessions: 4
Prerequisites: All 100 series courses.

CE-315 Application Practice Lab
Each participant has 20 minutes to coach, be coached and write a case study on an observed coaching session. Coach-the-coach occurs by faculty; feedback focuses on the development of the core coaching skills. Each participant must coach, be coached and write a case study to receive credit for this course.
Number of students: 16
Number of class sessions: 8
Prerequisites: 100 series courses and CE-310 Situational Coaching.

CE-320 Establishing Yourself As a Coach
Coaching is now found inside organizations as well as in multi-coach coaching groups, and individual coaching businesses. This module is designed to help establish yourself as a coach during for your first three to 18 months of coaching. This module will cover what you need to establish yourself as a coach, introduce you to the new coachee process, and teach you the hallmarks of achieving on-going coaching success.
Number of class sessions: 8
Prerequisites: All 100 series courses.

CE-325 Coaching Services Packet Project Lab
The objective of this module is to complete your coaching services package (welcome package) and course worksheets. By the end of 4 weeks, you must submit the project to faculty to receive credit for the course.
Number of students: 16
Number of class sessions: 4
Prerequisites:: 100 series courses and CE-320 Establishing Yourself as a Coach.

CE-410 Coach's Personal Foundation - Level 1
The first level of personal foundation focuses on the outer "package" that a person presents, identifying some of the most immediate roadblocks to moving forward. You will learn how to eliminate those roadblocks to personal growth, improve your attitude and create new and healthy habits, which support you in making choices that are more aligned to your true self.
Number of class sessions: 8
Prerequisites: All 100 series courses.

SECTION 8

Advanced Coaching Program Courses

Required Courses:

A-420 Coach's Personal Foundation - Level 2
The second level of personal foundation focuses on the inner "you"; what is most easily understood, "who" you really are. The WHO contains your being, your source for all else, and your place of personal awareness. All shifts and solutions begin at your WHO.
Number of class sessions: 8
Prerequisites: The Core Essentials program must be completed

A-430 Coach's Personal Foundation - Level 3
The third component of personal foundation is the set of processes, methods and values that drive our behavior – HOW we do the things, and HOW we are WHO we are. The fuel for the HOW of us is the WHO, which essentially yields the WHAT. The practical and application sides of learning and growth happen in the HOW. We begin the learning in the WHO and then apply it in the HOW. The actual "work" of personal development most likely happens here, and most directly affects individual growth. This is where new actions and skills are practiced, cementing new behaviors.
Number of class sessions: 8
Prerequisites: The Core Essentials program and A-420 Coach's Personal Foundation - Level 2.

A-435 Personal Foundation Practice Lab
In this entirely experiential course each participant will coach and receive feedback from the faculty and a peer, as well as completing a self-evaluation. The feedback will be used to guide their further training and development coaching on personal foundation issues. Coach-the-coach occurs by faculty. Each participant must coach, be coached and write a case study to receive credit for this course.
Number of Students: 16 students
Number of class sessions: 8
Prerequisites: The Core Essentials program, A-420 Coach's

Personal Foundation - Level 2 and A-430 Coach's Personal Foundation - Level 3.

A-601 Business Coaching Conversation

Business coaching really means coaching the people who can influence the performance, growth and development of the business. You will be able to more easily identify the focus of coaching required at any phase in the growth of a business, and how your own understanding of business influences your ability to coach people at the different phases.
Number of class sessions: 4
This is a required course in the ACP program and a prerequisite for all other advanced courses.
Prerequisites: The Core Essentials program.

A-701 Personal Coaching Conversation

Personal coaching is based on the level of trust and intimacy that exists between client and coach, and that the client has with him or herself. This course will improve your understanding of personal coaching and add to your comfort and competence doing personal coaching at different levels. You will develop a framework that allows you to coach people at any stage on their path of development, and realize how your own path influences your ability to coach others at different levels and stages.
Number of class sessions: 4
This is a required course in the ACP program and a prerequisite for all other advanced courses.
Prerequisites: The Core Essentials program.

Elective Courses:

A-513 Organizational Development

This course covers organizational development from a coaching perspective, because coaches develop organizations one person, team or group at a time. You will explore the nature of organizational development and how you can influence the organization's ability to change, flex and lighten itself thereby strengthening the organization.
Number of class sessions: 4
Prerequisites: The Core Essentials program A-501 Corporate Conversation Model or A–601 Business Coaching

Conversation and A-701 Personal Coaching Conversation (ACP program).

A-525 Coaching The Executive Practice Lab
In this entirely experiential course, each participant will demonstrate coaching an executive client, receive feedback from the faculty and a peer and also complete a self-evaluation. The feedback offered will be used to guide their further training and development. Coach-the-coach occurs by faculty. Each participant must coach, be coached and write a case study to receive credit for this course
Number of students: 16
Number of class sessions: 8
Prerequisites: The Core Essentials program and A-501 Corporate Conversation Model or A–601 Business Coaching Conversation and A-701 Personal Coaching Conversation (ACP program).

A-530 Assessments for Coaching
This course explores an assortment of assessments that coaches use to support different client needs. The coach will identify appropriate instruments such as Multirater 360°, DISC® and others to use in a variety of business situations.
Number of class sessions: 4
Prerequisites:: The Core Essentials program and A-501 Corporate Conversation Model or A–601 Business Coaching Conversation and A-701 Personal Coaching Conversation (ACP program).

A-610 New Business Success
Beginning a new business entails a variety of interesting challenges such as risk, personal growth, an extensive learning curve, potential errors in judgment, endless action steps to take and new levels of professional development. Learn about the steps and dynamics of starting up a new business, and discover the value of coaching in the start-up process.
Number of class sessions: 4
Prerequisites: The Core Essentials program and A-601 Business Coaching Conversation and A-701 Personal Coaching Conversation.

A-611 Small Business Success
The small business owner hires a coach to accelerate the company's growth and profitability. You will learn numerous

business principles, as well as the keys to small business success, which you can use to coach the small business owner to success. Given that many owners of small businesses have the characteristics and habits of entrepreneurs, beneficial coaching strategies related to these dynamic personalities will be explored.
Number of class sessions: 4
Prerequisites: The Core Essentials program and A-601 Business Coaching Conversation and A-701 Personal Coaching Conversation.

A-612 Business Turnarounds
You need to develop the ability to quickly size up the situation, discern the real problem sources, prioritize the work to be done, coach your client to immediate action and lay the groundwork for a profitable company. You will learn how to use the 'edge' in coaching interactions where there may be resistance to taking the sometimes radical, drastic or unusual actions that are required for a quick turnaround.
Number of class sessions: 4
Prerequisites: The Core Essentials program and A-601 Business Coaching Conversation and A-701 Personal Coaching Conversation.

A-620 Marketing
Marketing includes networking, referral-based marketing, niche identification, innovation, and the value-added approach. Learn how a company or business can use the principals of attraction to become irresistibly attractive to ideal customers, strengthen customer loyalty and and build a strong reputation by demonstrating mastery in one's profession, service or product line.
Number of class sessions: 4
Prerequisites: The Core Essentials program and A-601 Business Coaching Conversation and A-701 Personal Coaching Conversation.

A-621 Profitability
One of the main purposes in business is to make a profit. This course examines the main theories of profitability, what profitability means in regard to a successful coaching interaction with a business and various methods for measuring increased profitability. You will learn how to support a business from a coaching perspective in substantially increasing their profits.

Number of class sessions: 4
Prerequisites: The Core Essentials program and A-601 Business Coaching Conversation and A-701 Personal Coaching Conversation.

A-635 Coaching The Professional Practice Lab
In this entirely experiential course, each participant will demonstrate coaching a professional client, receive feedback from the faculty and a peer and also complete a self-evaluation. The feedback offered will be used to guide their further training and development.
Number of students: 16
Number of class sessions: 8
Prerequisites: The Core Essentials program and A-501 Corporate Conversation Model and A-701 Personal Coaching Conversation.

A-636 Coaching The Entrepreneur Practice Lab
In this entirely experiential course, each participant will demonstrate coaching a client who is an entrepreneur, receive feedback from the faculty and a peer and also complete a self-evaluation. The feedback offered will be used to guide their further training and development.
Number of students: 16
Number of class sessions: 8
Prerequisites: The Core Essentials program and A-501 Corporate Conversation Model and A-701 Personal Coaching Conversation.

A-637 Coaching The Manager Practice Lab
In this entirely experiential course, each participant will demonstrate coaching a client who is a manager, receive feedback from the faculty and a peer and also complete a self-evaluation. The feedback offered to the participant will be used to guide their further training and development. The feedback offered will be used to guide their further training and development.
Number of students: 16
Number of class sessions: 8
Prerequisites: The Core Essentials program and A-501 Corporate Conversation Model and A-701 Personal Coaching Conversation.

A-638 Coaching The Sales Professional Practice Lab

In this entirely experiential course, each participant will demonstrate coaching a client who is a sales professional, receive feedback from the faculty and a peer and also complete a self-evaluation. The feedback offered to the participant will be used to guide their further training and development.

Number of students: 16

Number of class sessions: 8

Prerequisites: The Core Essentials program and A-501 Corporate Conversation Model and A-701 Personal Coaching Conversation.

A-710 Life Planning

Life planning is the process by which a person consciously designs his or her own life instead of living by default. This course particularly focuses on how to structure a comprehensive coaching approach in four major areas; values and goals, mission, life map and Coach U's Clean Sweep program.

Number of class sessions: 4

Prerequisites: The Core Essentials program and A-601 Business Coaching Conversation and A-701 Personal Coaching Conversation.

A-711 Spiritual Path

Spirituality is the notion that we are all one, connected somehow with every other human being, yet distinct in our own gifts, views, direction and choices. This course supports the view that everybody has their own unique version of spirituality and has the ability to develop their spirituality by conscious effort. Other areas of focus are universal laws, the concept of surrender and the experience of bliss and fulfillment.

Number of class sessions: 4

Prerequisites: The Core Essentials program and A-601 Business Coaching Conversation and A-701 Personal Coaching Conversation.

A-712 Intuition

Intuition is the human capacity to know without the use of rational processes or concrete information. Learn to identify, sort and effectively act on information coming to you in an intuitive way.

Number of class sessions: 4
Prerequisites: The Core Essentials program and A-601 Business Coaching Conversation and A-701 Personal Coaching Conversation.

A-720 Financial Independence
Financial independence is achieved when you have more than enough money to live on now and for the rest of your life, and where your choices and goals are not influenced by the need to make money. This course helps you understand financial independence as a real possibility, not a pipe dream or source of disappointment, and that there as many ways to attain financial independence as there are people to dream them up. You will learn how to move through resistance to being financially independent and how to make the shifts and changes necessary to have financial independence be more than just a conversation.
Number of class sessions: 4
Prerequisites: The Core Essentials program and A-601 Business Coaching Conversation and A-701 Personal Coaching Conversation.

A-730 Attraction
Attraction is about being whole and present, so you effortlessly draw to you what you want in life, versus having to sell, seduce or promote yourself. You will come to fully understand the principles of attraction, and learn what is required to become irresistibly attractive, which will get you more of what you want and less of what you don't want in your life.
Number of class sessions: 8
Prerequisites: The Core Essentials program and A-601 Business Coaching Conversation and A-701 Personal Coaching Conversation.

A-745 Personal Path Practice Lab
In this entirely experiential course, based on the Personal Path Assessment, each participant will coach and receive feedback on their current demonstration of ability from the faculty, a peer and a self-evaluation. The feedback offered to the participant will be used to guide their further training and development.
16 students
Number of class sessions: 4
Prerequisites: The Core Essentials program and A-601 Business

Coaching Conversation and A-701 Personal Coaching Conversation.

A-746 Buff Practice Lab

In this entirely experiential course, based on the Buff Checklist, each participant will coach and receive feedback on their current demonstration of ability from the faculty, a peer and a self-evaluation. The feedback offered to the participant will be used to guide their further training and development.
16 students
Number of class sessions: 8
Prerequisites: The Core Essentials program, A-601 Business Coaching Conversation and A-701 Personal Coaching Conversation.

A-747 Restorative Practice Lab

In this entirely experiential course, you will experience real-time coaching drawing the distinctions out between coaching and therapy, and develop your ability to discern the difference. Each participant will coach and receive feedback on their current demonstration of ability from the faculty, a peer and a self-evaluation. The feedback offered to the participant will be used to guide their further training and development.
16 students
Number of class sessions: 8
Prerequisites: The Core Essentials program, A-601 Business Coaching Conversation and A-701 Personal Coaching Conversation.

A-810 Creating the Vision

The emphasis is on developing the professional by developing the person. The coach literally builds one's business "from the inside out." We'll consider a number of topics, which will enable you to ultimately establish a powerful and compelling vision for your business.
Number of class sessions: 4
Prerequisites: The Core Essentials program.

A-811 Exploding Myths

This course will challenge and inspire you to examine your personal foundation of beliefs and assumptions about being in business and what it means to be successful. Learn to zero in on the most significant opportunities to reframe limiting beliefs and behavior.

Number of class sessions: 4
Prerequisites: The Core Essentials program.

A-820 Marketing and Selling – Private Life Coaching Practice
This course is focused on building your practice through attraction-based marketing. Attraction is the result of offering high value, being someone worth hiring and knowing how to present yourself and your message. Learn how to attract ideal clients to your practice. Because coaching is just an interesting idea to potential clients until they actually hire you, learn proven ways to share the coaching message and to "coach" the client to say "Yes!"
Number of class sessions: 4
Prerequisites: The Core Essentials program.

A-821 Marketing and Selling – External Corporate/Business Practice
Marketing and sales skills are critical to getting your product to the organizational clients you target. As a coach and businessperson, you must establish your target market and develop a sales process that will attract clients so you can get on to the business of coaching!
Number of class sessions: 4
Prerequisites: The Core Essentials program.

A-830 Practice Management – Private Life Coaching Practice
A coaching practice is a business that is only as good as your ability to deliver quality coaching and manage all aspects of your coaching company. The client relies on the coach to provide the structure necessary to continue to improve, even in the midst of distractions, diversions, "better ideas" and new priorities. Learn to provide plenty of support without crowding the client or creating a dependency. Learn additional steps required to own and run a successful coaching practice.
Number of class sessions: 4
Prerequisites: The Core Essentials program.

A-831 Practice Management – External Corporate/Business Practice
Although each external coach is responsible for unique issues within his or her practice, all coaches share general business concerns that are critical to a successful practice. This course addresses issues in practice management including how to start, build, and operate a professional coaching practice.

Number of class sessions: 4
Prerequisites: The Core Essentials program.

A-835 Strong Start Beginner Practice Lab
This entirely experiential course supports new coaches in the mechanics of beginning to coach professionally, focusing on each participant's need, and how they intend to coach. This course is run much like a group coaching experience where each individual can explore their specific challenges and receive coaching by faculty and peers. This is a fully participatory course for individuals who are ready to take action.
Number of class sessions: 8
Prerequisites: The Core Essentials program.

A-840 Integrating/Marketing Group Coaching
Group coaching can provide a means to diversify your coaching product offerings. In this course you will determine the value of group coaching to your particular client market and learn how to fully integrate group coaching into an existing coaching practice. This course also discusses the most successful methods for marketing group coaching.
Number of class sessions: 4
Prerequisites: The Core Essentials program.

A-841 Integrating/Marketing Teleclasses
TeleClasses can provide a means to diversify your coaching product offerings. In this course you will explore the dynamics of a valuable TeleClass experience, and the types of TeleClasses most beneficial to your particular client market. You will also learn how to fully integrate TeleClasses into your existing coaching practice. This course also discusses the most successful methods for marketing TeleClasses.
Number of class sessions: 4
Prerequisites: The Core Essentials program.

A-850 Transitioning to Full Time Coaching
Most individuals find it challenging to transition to having a financially successful, full-time coaching practice. Learn the three basic strategies to transitioning from full time job to full time coach.
Number of class sessions: 4
Prerequisites: The Core Essentials program.

A-851 Advanced Practice Development

Participants will examine advanced practice development topics, including the attitudes, skills and behaviors needed to create and maintain a full coaching practice. A coach who has a waiting list feels completely free to strongly coach the current clients, which is exactly what they need. Learn the strategies for developing and maintaining a full coaching practice, which mesh with your personal and professional strengths and interests.
Number of class sessions: 4
Prerequisites: The Core Essentials program.

A-855 Strong Start Advanced Practice Lab

This completely experiential course supports coaches who have some experience coaching and running their professional businesses. This course is run much like a group coaching experience where each individual can explore his or her individual needs, particular challenges and coaching style, and receive specific coaching by faculty and their peers. This is a fully participatory course geared for individuals ready to take specific action to move to the next place professionally.
Number of students: 16
Number of class sessions: 8
Prerequisites: The Core Essentials program and A-835 Strong Start Beginner Practice Lab, and 100 coaching hours and have coached at least 15 different coachees.

A-865 Million Dollar Coach Forum

This participatory course supports the experienced coach who has reached a high level of success and wants to explore the million-dollar game. Coaches must be earning a six-figure income through their coaching practices to enroll in this course. This course is not for the inexperienced coach who is just interested in the conversation.
Number of class sessions: 8
Prerequisites: The Core Essentials program.

A-910 Overview/New Skills for Group Coaching

Group coaching is defined as coaching with two or more people simultaneously. Learn the skills, tools and strategies to successfully provide group coaching. Be prepared to fully participate in this course and practice this refined coaching skill set.

Number of class sessions: 4
Prerequisites: The Core Essentials program, A-601 Business Coaching Conversation and A-701 Personal Coaching Conversation.

A-912 Overview/New Skills for Teleclass Leading
TeleClasses offer a unique environment for learning that support a popular coaching model. Since many coaches have global practices, TeleClasses can replace on site or in person workshops to some degree. Learn the skills, tools and strategies to successfully create and conduct TeleClasses. Be prepared to fully participate in the course and practice being a TeleClass leader.
Number of class sessions: 4
Prerequisites: The Core Essentials program, A-601 Business Coaching Conversation and A-701 Personal Coaching Conversation.

A-920 Coaching The Essence
Coaching the essence describes coaching that is direct, succinct, and quickly gives a client additional clarity on major issues. With a good skill set, intuition, instinct, insight, and trust in the client, you can ask big questions, make significant observations candidly and non-judgmentally, and easily coach a client's important issues.
Number of students: 16
Number of class sessions: 8
Prerequisites: The Core Essentials program, A-601 Business Coaching Conversation and A-701 Personal Coaching Conversation.

A-925 Advanced Coaching Skills Practice Lab
Each participant has 20 minutes to coach, be coached and write a case study on an observed coaching session. Coach-the-coach occurs by faculty; feedback focuses on the development of the core coaching skills. Each participant must coach, be coached and write a case study to receive credit for this course.
Number of students: 16
Number of class sessions: 8
Prerequisites: The Core Essentials program, A-601 Business Coaching Conversation and A-701 Personal Coaching Conversation.

A-935 Group Coaching Practice Lab
An entirely experiential course focused on each individual's coaching ability and skill in running specifically directed group coaching interactions. Each participant will coach and receive feedback on their current demonstration of ability from the faculty, a peer and a self-evaluation. The feedback offered will be used to guide their further training and development.
Number of students: 16
Number of class sessions: 8
Prerequisites: The Core Essentials program, A-601 Business Coaching Conversation, A-701 Personal Coaching Conversation and A-910 Overview/New Skills for Group Coaching.

A-945 Teleclass Leading Practice Lab
An entirely experiential course that is focused on each individual's coaching ability and skill in running a specifically directed TeleClass. Each participant will coach and receive feedback on their current demonstration of ability from the faculty, a peer and a self-evaluation. The feedback offered will be used to guide their further training and development.
Number of students: 16
Number of class sessions: 8
Prerequisites: The Core Essentials program, A-601 Business Coaching Conversation, A-701 Personal Coaching Conversation and A-912 Overview/New Skills for TeleClass Leading.

A-950 Coaching for Therapists (ONLY)
Therapists make wonderful coaches, yet it can be a challenge to make the shift from being a therapist to being a coach. This course is offered as support, inspiration, and guidance for therapists who want to make the transition easier and more successful.
Number of class sessions: 4
Prerequisites: The Core Essentials program, A-601 Business Coaching Conversation and A-701 Personal Coaching Conversation.

SECTION 9

Advanced Corporate Coaching Program Courses

Core Courses:

A-445 Personal/Professional Foundation Practice Lab

In this entirely experiential course each participant will coach, be coached, and receive feedback from the faculty and a peer, as well as completing a self-evaluation. The feedback offered will be used to guide their further training and development coaching on personal foundation issues. Coach-the-coach occurs by faculty. Each participant must coach, be coached and write a case study to receive credit for this course.
Number of Students: 16
Number of class sessions: 8
Prerequisites: The Core Essentials program and CCU-05 Professional Foundations.

A-515 Corporate Conversation Model Practice Lab

In this experiential course each participant will coach and receive feedback from the faculty and a peer and as well as completing a self-evaluation. The feedback offered to the participant will be used to guide their further training and development. Coach-the-coach occurs by faculty. Each participant must coach, be coached and write a case study to receive credit for this course
Number of Students: 16
Number of class sessions: 8
Prerequisites: The Core Essentials program and Prerequisites: A-501 Corporate Conversation Model

A-501 Corporate Conversation Model
Every replicable approach has a model to ensure that the process works consistently. This course covers the model for coaching conversations and provides a process for establishing meaningful coaching relationships.

A-440 Professional Foundations
As coaches, we are sometimes asked to coach others around issues that we have not fully mastered ourselves. Professional Foundations invites self-exploration and self-development in areas that are important to our clients. By strengthening our professional foundations, we can serve as role models for clients who are working toward self-improvement goals.
Number of class sessions: 8

A-531 PCSI
The PCSI® is a coaching tool that helps coaches and clients understand how to connect more easily in coaching relationships. In this course, we examine the four PCSI styles and become aware of how these styles are expressed in the workplace. With a deeper understanding of styles, we can learn to flex our styles to support our clients.
Number of class sessions: 8
Prerequisites: For Advanced Corporate Coaching Program and A-501 Corporate Conversation Model

Elective Courses:

A-513 Organizational Development
This course covers organizational development from a coaching perspective, because coaches develop organizations one person, team or group at a time. You will explore the nature of organizational development and how you can influences the organization's ability to change, flex and lighten itself thereby strengthening the organization.
Number of class sessions: 4
Prerequisites: The Core Essentials program and A-501 Corporate Conversation Model or A–601 Business Coaching Conversation and A-701 Personal Coaching Conversation (ACP program).

A-525 Coaching The Executive Practice Lab
In this entirely experiential course, each participant will demonstrate coaching an executive client, receive feedback from the faculty and a peer and also complete a self-evaluation. The feedback offered will be used to guide their further training and development. Coach-the-coach occurs by faculty. Each participant must coach, be coached and write a case study to receive credit for this course
Number of students: 16
Number of class sessions: 8
Prerequisites: The Core Essentials program and A-501 Corporate Conversation Model or A–601 Business Coaching Conversation and A-701 Personal Coaching Conversation (ACP program).

A-635 Coaching The Professional Practice Lab
In this entirely experiential course, each participant will demonstrate coaching a professional client, receive feedback from the faculty and a peer and also complete a self-evaluation. The feedback offered will be used to guide their further training and development. Coach-the-coach occurs by faculty
Number of students: 16
Number of class sessions: 8
Prerequisites: The Core Essentials program and A-501 Corporate Conversation Model and A-701 Personal Coaching Conversation.

A-636 Coaching The Entrepreneur Practice Lab
In this entirely experiential course, each participant will demonstrate coaching a client who is an entrepreneur, receive feedback from the faculty and a peer and also complete a self-evaluation. The feedback offered will be used to guide their further training and development.
Number of students: 16
Number of class sessions: 8
Prerequisites: The Core Essentials program and A-501 Corporate Conversation Model and A-701 Personal Coaching Conversation.

A-637 Coaching The Manager Practice Lab
In this entirely experiential course, each participant will demonstrate coaching a client who is a manager, receive feedback from the faculty and a peer and also complete a

self-evaluation. The feedback offered to the participant will be used to guide their further training and development. The feedback offered will be used to guide their further training and development.
Number of students: 16
Number of class sessions: 8
Prerequisites: The Core Essentials program and A-501 Corporate Conversation Model and A-701 Personal Coaching Conversation.

A-638 Coaching The Sales Professional Practice Lab
In this entirely experiential course, each participant will demonstrate coaching a client who is a sales professional, receive feedback from the faculty and a peer and also complete a self-evaluation. The feedback offered to the participant will be used to guide their further training and development.
Number of students: 16
Number of class sessions: 8
Prerequisites: The Core Essentials program and A-501 Corporate Conversation Model and A-701 Personal Coaching Conversation.

A-810 Creating the Vision
The emphasis is on developing the professional by developing the person. The coach literally builds one's business "from the inside out." We'll consider a number of topics, which will enable you to ultimately establish a powerful and compelling vision for your business.
Number of class sessions: 4
Prerequisites: The Core Essentials program.

A-811 Exploding Myths
This course will challenge and inspire you to examine your personal foundation of beliefs and assumptions about being in business and what it means to be successful. Learn to zero in on the most significant opportunities to reframe limiting beliefs and behavior.
Number of class sessions: 4
Prerequisites: The Core Essentials program.

A-835 Strong Start Beginner Practice Lab
This entirely experiential course supports new coaches in the mechanics of beginning to coach professionally, focusing on each participant's need, and how they intend to coach. This

course is run much like a group coaching experience where each individual can explore their specific challenges and receive coaching by faculty and peers. This is a fully participatory course for individuals who are ready to take action.
Number of class sessions: 8
Prerequisites: The Core Essentials program.

A-840 Integrating/Marketing Group Coaching
Group coaching can provide a means to diversify your coaching product offerings. In this course you will determine the value of group coaching to your particular client market and learn how to fully integrate group coaching into an existing coaching practice. This course also discusses the most successful methods for marketing group coaching.
Number of class sessions: 4
Prerequisites: The Core Essentials program.

A-841 Integrating/Marketing Teleclasses
TeleClasses can provide a means to diversify your coaching product offerings. In this course you will explore the dynamics of a valuable TeleClass experience, and the types of TeleClasses most beneficial to your particular client market. You will also learn how to fully integrate TeleClasses into your existing coaching practice. This course also discusses the most successful methods for marketing TeleClasses.
Number of class sessions: 4
Prerequisites: The Core Essentials program.

A-850 Transitioning to Full Time Coaching
Most individuals find it challenging to transition to having a financially successful, full-time coaching practice. Learn the three basic strategies to transitioning from full time job to full time coach.
Number of class sessions: 4
Prerequisites: The Core Essentials program.

A-851 Advanced Practice Development
Participants will examine advanced practice development topics, including the attitudes, skills and behaviors needed to create and maintain a full coaching practice. A coach who has a waiting list of clients, feels completely free to strongly coach the current clients, which is exactly what they need. Learn the strategies for developing and maintaining a full

coaching practice, which mesh with your personal and professional strengths and interests.
Number of class sessions: 4
Prerequisites: The Core Essentials program.

A-855 Strong Start Advanced Practice Lab
This completely experiential course supports coaches who have some experience coaching and running their businesses. This course is run like a group coaching experience where each individual can explore his or her individual needs, challenges and coaching style, and receive specific coaching by faculty and their peers. This is a fully participatory course geared for individuals ready to take specific action to move to the next place professionally.
Number of students: 16
Number of class sessions: 8
Prerequisites: The Core Essentials program and A-835 Strong Start Beginner Practice Lab, and 100 coaching hours and have coached at least 15 different coachees.

A-865 Million Dollar Coach Forum
This participatory course supports the experienced coach who has reached a high level of success and wants to explore the million-dollar game. Coaches must be earning a six-figure income through their coaching practices to enroll in this course. This course is not for the inexperienced coach who is just interested in the conversation.
Number of class sessions: 8
Prerequisites: The Core Essentials program.

A-910 Overview/New Skills for Group Coaching
Group coaching is defined as coaching with two or more people simultaneously. Learn the skills, tools and strategies to successfully provide group coaching. Be prepared to fully participate in this course and practice this refined coaching skill set.
Number of class sessions: 4
Prerequisites: The Core Essentials program, A-601 Business Coaching Conversation and A-701 Personal Coaching Conversation.

A-912 Overview/New Skills for Teleclass Leading
TeleClasses offer a unique environment for learning that support a popular coaching model. Since many coaches have global practices, TeleClasses can replace on site or in

person workshops to some degree. Learn the skills, tools and strategies to successfully create and conduct TeleClasses. Be prepared to fully participate in the course and practice being a TeleClass leader.
Number of class sessions: 4
Prerequisites: The Core Essentials program, A-601 Business Coaching Conversation and A-701 Personal Coaching Conversation.

A-920 Coaching The Essence
Coaching the essence describes coaching that is direct, succinct, and quickly gives a client additional clarity on major issues. With a good skill set, intuition, instinct, insight, and trust in the client, you can ask big questions, make significant observations candidly and non-judgmentally, and easily coach a client's important issues.
Number of students: 16
Number of class sessions: 8
Prerequisites: The Core Essentials program, A-601 Business Coaching Conversation and A-701 Personal Coaching Conversation.

A-925 Advanced Coaching Skills Practice Lab
Each participant has 20 minutes to coach, be coached and write a case study on an observed coaching session. Coach-the-coach occurs by faculty; feedback focuses on the development of the core coaching skills. Each participant must coach, be coached and write a case study to receive credit for this course.
Number of students: 16
Number of class sessions: 8
Prerequisites: The Core Essentials program, A-601 Business Coaching Conversation and A-701 Personal Coaching Conversation.

A-935 Group Coaching Practice Lab
An entirely experiential course focused on each individual's coaching ability and skill in running specifically directed group coaching interactions. Each participant will coach and receive feedback on their current demonstration of ability from the faculty, a peer and a self-evaluation. The feedback offered will be used to guide their further training and development.
Number of students: 16
Number of class sessions: 8

Prerequisites: The Core Essentials program, A-601 Business Coaching Conversation, A-701 Personal Coaching Conversation and A-910 Overview/New Skills for Group Coaching.

A-945 Teleclass Leading Practice Lab

An entirely experiential course that is focused on each individual's coaching ability and skill in running a specifically directed TeleClass. Each participant will coach and receive feedback on their current demonstration of ability from the faculty, a peer and a self-evaluation. The feedback offered will be used to guide their further training and development.
Number of students: 16
Number of class sessions: 8
Prerequisites: The Core Essentials program, A-601 Business Coaching Conversation, A-701 Personal Coaching Conversation and A-912 Overview/New Skills for TeleClass Leading.

A-821 Marketing & Selling (External Coaches)

Marketing and sales skills are critical to getting your product to the organizational clients you target. As a coach and businessperson, you must establish your target market and develop a sales process that will attract clients... so you can get on to the business of coaching!
Number of class sessions: 4

A-822 Marketing & Selling (Internal Coaches)

Marketing, more than any aspect of the corporate decision-making process, is often misunderstood. Marketing and sales skills are necessary to extend coaching and establish its value within your organization, while competing with internal budget limitations and other issues. As a coach and employee, you must identify your internal target market and develop a sales process that will attract clients... so you can get on to the business of coaching!
Number of class sessions: 4

A-831 Practice Management (External Coaches)

Although each external coach is responsible for unique issues within his or her practice, all coaches share general business concerns that are critical to a successful practice. This course addresses issues in practice management including how to start, build, and operate a professional coaching practice.
Number of class sessions: 4

A-832 Program Management (Internal Coaches)
Internal coaches are challenged to build an effective program while managing the cultural, political and organizational nuances within the organization. This course addresses the processes and issues to consider when developing a coaching program within a company.
Number of class sessions: 4

A-510 Context for Collaboration
Today's business environment is leaner with increased reliance on individuals to contribute to the success of the organization. With less top-down leadership and more pressure to perform, individuals and teams are learning the value of collaboration in the workforce. Coaches are ideally positioned to model a collaborative approach to achieving extraordinary business results.
Number of class sessions: 4
Prerequisites: A-501 Corporate Conversation Model

A-511 Special Topics in Corporate Coaching
Many believe that there is a crisis of commitment in today's organizations. Rampant downsizing, career uncertainty, and lack of ethical responsibility, have contributed to a deep sense of resignation and demoralization among employees, which greatly impacts productivity and the bottom line. Also, our world has broadened from a local marketplace to a global business arena. As our business borders blur, the increasingly diverse workforce impacts the social and financial well-being of a corporation. The course explores the coach's role in revitalizing the workplace, and also the challenges and opportunities of diversity and the issues that coaches may encounter.
Prerequisites: A-501 Corporate Conversation Model

A-530 Assessments for Coaching
This course explores assessments that coaches use to support different client needs,, as well as the coach's role in administering multirater (360°) assessments and the coach approach to delivering feedback.
Prerequisites: A-501 Corporate Conversation Model

.

A-514 Coaching Business Teams
In today's business environment, teams must quickly negotiate the natural stages of team development and deliver unprecedented high levels of performance. In this course, the coach will develop a toolkit with which to support teams.
Number of class sessions: 4
Prerequisites: A-501 Corporate Conversation Model

SECTION 10

The International Coach Federation (ICF)

The International Coach Federation (ICF) is the largest non-profit professional association worldwide of personal and business coaches, with more than 8000 members, and over 130 chapters in more than 30 countries. The ICF exists to build, support and preserve the integrity of the coaching profession around the globe. The ICF supports and fosters development of the coaching profession; has programs to maintain and upgrade the standards of the profession; conducts a certification program that is the gold standard for coaches worldwide; and conducts the world's premier conference and other educational events for coaches.

To preserve the integrity of the coaching profession, the ICF is actively involved in researching and developing programs in the legal, regulatory, and credentialing areas that will serve coaches and their coachees. In 2002, the ICF adopted an Ethical Conduct Review (ECR) Policy that provides for review, investigation and response to alleged unethical practices or behavior deviating from the established ICF Ethical Guidelines. This policy provides a forum where the public can bring complaints about alleged unethical conduct by ICF members or ICF credentialed coaches. The ICF is committed to a 'model of excellence'.

CoachInc.com recognizes the importance of credentialing with ICF and supports and facilitates the process by providing CoachInc.com certifications. (See information on Coach U and Corporate Coach U certifications in Section 11).

The Purpose of the ICF Credentialing Program is:

1. Establish and administer minimum standards for credentialing professional coaches and coach training agencies.
2. Assure the public that participating coaches and coach training programs meet or exceed these minimum standards.
3. Reinforce professional coaching as a distinct and self-regulating profession.

The ICF credential is awarded to professional coaches and coach training programs who meet or exceed these minimum standards. To ensure every applicant receives a fair and unbiased evaluation, Master Certified Coaches are randomly selected to individually review, evaluate, and rate applications. Their ratings are used to make a final determination regarding the credential.

The evaluation process relies heavily upon an applicant's documentation of the following:

- Attendance at a formally accredited coach training program like Coach U's Advanced Coaching Program (ACP) or Corporate Coach U's Advanced Corporate Coaching Program (ACCP).
- Successfully applied coach training and skill with coachees.

ICF Certifications, Designations and Key Terms

Associated Certified Coach (ACC) requires:

- Coach-Specific Training Hours: 60
- Client Coaching Hours Experience: 100
- CoachInc.com Training Programs to provide coach-specific training hours:
  - Core Essentials Program (CEP)
  - Core Essentials Fast Track Program (CEFTP)
  - Advanced Coaching Program (ACP)

  - Advanced Corporate Coaching Program (ACCP)

Professional Certified Coach (PCC) requires:

- Coach-Specific Training Hours: 125
- Client Coaching Hours Experience: 750
- CoachInc.com Programs to provide coach-specific training hours <u>via the Portfolio Track</u>:
  - Coach U's Advanced Coaching Program (ACP)
  - Corporate Coach U's Advanced Corporate Coaching Program (ACCP)
- CoachInc.com T raining Programs to apply <u>via the ACTP Track</u>:
  - The Advanced Coaching Program (ACP) then the Coach U Certified Graduate (CUCG) requirements; or
  - The Advanced Corporate Coaching Program (ACCP) then the Corporate Coach U Certified Graduate (CCUCG) requirements

Master Certified Coach (MCC) requires:

- Coach-Specific Training Hours: 200
- Coachee Coaching Hours Experience: 2500
- CoachInc.com Training Programs to provide coach-specific training hours <u>via the Portfolio Track</u>:
  - Coach U's Advanced Coaching Program (ACP)
  - Corporate Coach U's Advanced Corporate Coaching Program (ACCP)
- CoachInc.com Programs to apply <u>via the ACTP Track</u>:
  - The Advanced Coaching Program (ACP) then the Coach U Certified Graduate (CUCG) requirements; or
  - The Advanced Corporate Coaching Program (ACCP) then the Corporate Coach U Certified Graduate (CCUCG) requirements

Accredited Coach Training Program (ACTP) designates training organizations that are aligned with the ICF's definition of professional coaching and the ICF 'Pledge of Ethics' and 'Standards of Ethical Conduct' and whose methods, processes and/or techniques for Professional Coaching and/or testing, have been reviewed and approved by the ICF.

Student Contact Learning Hours
(SCLH) - The time a student is engaged in coach specific training (does not include lunch or break time).

Coach Specific Training
Coach-Specific Training is training that is predominantly marketed as exclusively teaching and applying coaching skills in a manner consistent with the ICF Core Competencies.

Client/Coachee Coaching Hours
For purposes of individual credentialing for ACC, PCC and MCC, a coaching hour is 60 minutes coaching time with a person who has hired you as a coach, with whom you have a formal coaching agreement, and who you coach rather than providing any other service such as consulting or therapy. If you perform coaching and other services for a coachee, you may only count the actual time spent coaching toward certification. You may not count time providing other services.

International Coach Federation
2365 Harrodsburg Road
Suite A325
Lexington, KY 40504-3335 USA
Toll-free: 1-888-423-3131
Direct: 1-859-219-3580
Fax: 859-226-4411
icfoffice@coachfederation.org
www.coachfederation.org

SECTION 11

CoachInc.Com Certification And Accreditation

CoachInc.com recognizes the importance of credentialing and offers ICF Accredited Coach Training Programs (ACTP). Obtaining the Coach U (CUCG) or Corporate Coach U (CCUCG) certification designations facilitates and expedites obtaining ICF certification.

Coach U's Advanced Coaching Program (ACP) is an ICF ACTP approved program and offers the Coach U Certified Graduate (CUCG) designation, and Corporate Coach U's Advanced Corporate Coaching Program (ACCP) is an ICF approved program and offers the Corporate Coach U Certified Graduate (CCUCG) designation.

Completing the certification requirements and obtaining the CCUG or CCUCG designation allows you to apply for ICF certification via the ACTP Track. If you meet the ICF requirements for credentialing without completing an ICF ACTP approved program, you would need to apply for ICF certification through the Portfolio Track.

SECTION 12

Coaching Is Global

We have students and/or graduates in the following countries:

- Australia
- Austria
- Bahamas
- Belgium
- Bermuda
- Brazil
- Bulgaria
- Canada
- China
- Columbia
- Cyprus
- Denmark
- Egypt
- Finland
- France
- Germany
- Hong Kong
- India
- Indonesia
- Ireland
- Israel
- Italy
- Jamaica
- Japan
- Kenya
- Liechtenstein
- Malaysia
- Mexico
- Netherlands
- New Zealand
- Norway
- Philippines
- Poland
- Puerto Rico
- Romania
- Russia
- Singapore
- South Africa
- South Korea
- Spain
- Sweden
- Switzerland
- Taiwan
- Thailand
- United Arab Emirates
- United Kingdom
- United States
- Venezuela
- Virgin Islands

SECTION 13

How To Contact Us

For general or enrollment information, please contact us as indicated below. If you visit our web sites and click on Programs & Services, most of your questions and concerns will be addressed. However, please feel free to contact us directly.

If you reside in the US, Canada or a country not listed below contact:

Coach U, Inc.
PO Box 512, Andover, KS, 67002, USA
Toll Free Phone: 1-888-857-6410
Toll Free Fax: 1-888-857-6410
Phone: 1-920-834-9663 (for callers outside of North America)
Fax: 1-316-733-1760
Email: admissions@coachinc.com
URL: http://www.coachu.com

Corporate Coach U, Inc.
P.O. Box 881595, Steamboat Springs, CO, 80488-1588, USA
Toll Free Phone: 1-888-857-6410
Toll Free Fax: 1-888-857-6410
Phone: 1-920-834-9663 (for callers outside of North America)
Fax: 1-508-533-9012
Email: admissions@coachinc.com
URL: http://www.ccui.com

If you reside in the UK or Europe contact:

Coach U Europe
248 Walsall Road
Bridgetown, Cannock, Staffordshire, WS11 0JL, U.K.
Phone: Toll Free UK 0800 0854 317
Toll Free from most European Countries 00800 0792 6247
Alternative number +44 (0) 870 751 8824
Fax: +44 (0) 870 7518829
Email: info@coachueurope.com or
euroenquiries@coachu.com
URL: http://www.coachueurope.com

If you reside in Australia or New Zealand contact:

Coach U Australia & New Zealand Pty Ltd.
PO Box 868, Miranda 2232, NSW Australia
Phone: +61 2 9542 5888
Fax: +61 2 9542 5588
Email: info@coachuoz.com.au or
coachuoz@coachuoz.com.au
URL: http://www.coachuoz.com.au

If you reside in Italy and speak Italian, contact:

Corporate Coach U Italia
Piazza Borromeo, 10
20123 MILANO
Email: info@coachuitalia.com
URL: http://www.coachuitalia.com

If you reside in Japan, contact:

Coach 21
13-3 Ichiban-chyo, Chiyoda-ku, Tokyo 102-0082, Japan
Phone: 03-3237-9781
Fax: 03-3237-8814
Email: hirano@coach.co.jp
URL: http://www.coach.co.jp

If you reside in Korea, contact:

CCU Korea
Nonhyun-dong 88-9, Jeil Building 3F, Kangnam-ku, Seoul, Korea
Phone: 02-2106-4029
Fax: 02-2106-4001
Email: Gene@eklc.co.kr
URL: http://www.eklc.co.kr

If you reside in Singapore or Asia contact:

CoachHouse Asia (HQ-Singapore)
9 Bishan Place, #06-05Junction 8, Singapore 579837
Phone: (65) 625-COACH (625-26224)
Email: info@coachhouseasia.com
URL: http://www.coachhouseasia.com

NOTES